CULTURE SHOCK!

Czech Republic

Tim Nollen

Graphic Arts Center Publishing Company
Portland, Oregon

In the same series

Australia	India	Philippines	London at Your Door
Bolivia	Indonesia	Singapore	Paris at Your Door
Borneo	Ireland	South Africa	Rome at Your Door
Britain	Israel	Spain	
Burma	Italy	Sri Lanka	A Globe-Trotter's Guide
California	Japan	Sweden	A Parent's Guide
Canada	Korea	Switzerland	A Student's Guide
Chile	Laos	Syria	A Traveller's Medical Guide
China	Malaysia	Taiwan	A Wife's Guide
Cuba	Mauritius	Thailand	Living and Working Abroad
Denmark	Mexico	Turkey	Working Holidays Abroad
Egypt	Morocco	UAE	
France	Nepal	USA	
Germany	Netherlands	USA—The	
Greece	Norway	South	
Hong Kong	Pakistan	Vietnam	

Illustrations by TRIGG
Photographs from Tim Nollen

This book is published by special
arrangement with Times Editions Pte Ltd
Times Centre, 1 New Industrial Road, Singapore 536196
International Standard Book Number 1-55868-303-8
Library of Congress Catalog Number 96-77209
Graphic Arts Center Publishing Company
P.O. Box 10306 • Portland, Oregon 97296-0306 • (503) 226-2402

Printed in Singapore

Prague Castle Gardens – the lion is on the Czech national seal.

CONTENTS

ACKNOWLEDGEMENTS

Like so many other foreigners I've met in the Czech Republic, my first taste of the land and the people in 1991 was thrilling and intriguing. Something in the people resonated wonderfully well with me—I found myself naturally drawn into the culture and society, and, having come for a short stay, I find myself still here several years later. It has not been all rosy as it seems in retrospect, of course—culture shock for me took on many guises of frustration and boredom, yet as I worked on this book I was able to see clearly why I love this country: it is simply a beautiful, rich, and endearing place.

Many thanks are due to everyone who has helped me and this book along the way: in roughly chronological order this includes: the staff at SFC and at SPUSA who helped me get my feet on the ground; Aleš Bílek, Aleš Kaňka, Jarmila Kotůlková, Ludmila Šímková, and the Holeňa family; Iva Juřičková; Honza Jančar and family; Luboš Ziegler and Bobo; Karel and Eva Pulkrabovi; everyone at PRS, especially Michele Van Saun and Pepa Toul, David Biskup, Jiří Flaks; Pat Hertel; Jiří Navrátil; Kelly Joyce; those who aided in the research of this book: Jonathan Griffiths for the contact and assistance, Steve Setian, Chris DesForges, Ekko Kisjes and Janny, Hans-Peter Grimm, Martin Stanley, Odile Cisneros, David deVries, Guillaume Bastard, Leandro Palazolo, Joanne Clarke, Anděla Malá; and most of all, Mom, Dad and 'Tine.

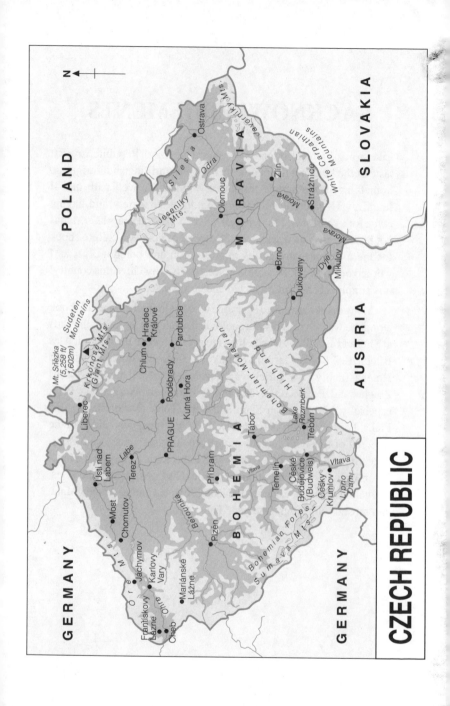

CZECH REPUBLIC

INTRODUCTION

Czechs are relatively unknown outside their own country, so most people coming to the Czech Republic for the first time have little or no idea what to expect. As a small nation located in the heart of central Europe, the Czech lands have experienced an extraordinarily rich cultural development—and a tumultuous political history, particularly in this century. Forty-one years of Communism came abruptly to an end with the November 1989 'Velvet Revolution,' and since then the Czech lands have enjoyed an exuberant, refreshing, and often complicated independence. The transformation to a democratic society has brought about fundamental change to the people, yet through it all the Czechs retain a unique pride and a humble zest for life.

Getting to know the Czechs and their culture can be an enriching, if at times trying experience. The purpose of this book is to help you anticipate the differences you will encounter, and ultimately help you not only appreciate these – be they joys or difficulties – but come to love them. You'll probably find, as most long term foreign residents do, that when the time comes to leave you won't want to go.

ORGANISATION OF THE BOOK

This book is about living in the Czech Republic, as opposed to travelling here. Its emphasis is on the people themselves: after providing a brief historical background, we dive right into the heart and soul of the Czech character and temperament. Using this as a basis, we proceed to describe social organisation and family life. As most people coming to the country are involved in business, we give a thorough account of standard business practices and how these can differ from what you may be used to. The rest of the book is concerned with practical matters of communicating, socialising, experiencing Czech culture, and dealing with all the nuts and bolts of settling in, from finding a home to setting up a bank account to sending the kids to school.

It's not always easy, but we hope that through this insider's introduction to the people, you'll gain an insight to the intriguing and beguiling world of the Czechs.

WHAT IS CULTURE SHOCK?

The most exciting thing about spending any period of time in a foreign country is getting to know the people, and this indeed is the 'culture shock' – the adaptation to foreign customs, mannerisms, and traditions. Living in the Czech Republic can be thrilling, beautiful, and enriching beyond anything you could imagine but it can also be frustrating, grey, and difficult if you don't approach it with an eager and open mind.

Because the task of relocating can be so logistically complicated and, at times, emotionally overwhelming, it is important to be aware of the culture to which you are moving; that's why this book came into being. The name, Culture Shock, is a real emotional state that one goes through when adjusting to a different culture. This can be a very sensitive thing – sometimes you don't realise why you get frustrated all of a sudden, or why you find yourself blatantly criticising those around you. What's shocking about it is that it can be so subtle, and you'll have a hard time recognising the symptoms.

The stages of culture shock are usually described as going from euphoria in the first month or two, to a rather sudden low period during the third to sixth month or so, to a gradual reawakening to your new country, with a stronger sense of confidence and energy. These time periods can vary considerably, and they can even recur during the stay.

The initial excitement of moving to a foreign country is what brings about the euphoria and, especially in a city like Prague, you'll undoubtedly find yourself walking on clouds. Everything is so new that you see every day as an adventure.

By the time your daily routine is established, you've become more familiar with the difficulties of communicating in a strange language, of not being able to get your favourite coffee, and of being away from your friends at home. There will be times when you find yourself criticizing little things, blaming them on your host people, and not understanding why you're so down all the time. If you arrive in the Czech Republic in the fall, this can be particularly hazardous, as winters here are long.

There is a useful and important defence against this blackness: don't start questioning yourself, and don't start lashing out at these strange customs and mannerisms. Just realise that this is a common, cyclical experience that everyone goes through in one form or another and therefore don't let yourself get too down when the going gets tough. Continue to approach with an open and eager mind: to progress in learning about the culture, in language study, and in new friend-ships as much as possible. Try not to spend too much time with other expatriates complaining about the differences, even though this is easy to do and can help in letting off steam. This down phase can be very deceptive: it's not really a depression or a shock, it's a frustration and a confusion, which can take any form of mildness or severity. This is the hardest time but it will pass. Those who give up during the low period and go home often regret it later.

By the sixth to ninth month or so, you've lived through the hard times and you'll 'suddenly' realise that you can speak some Czech, that you have some good friends and colleagues, and that you know something about the culture, and this is really what the experience of living abroad is about. Most people find that by the end of the first year, they are finally beginning to really know the culture. A deeper understanding then takes place during the second year and beyond.

— Chapter One —

HISTORY AND POLITICS

WHO ARE THE CZECHS?

The words 'Bohemia' and 'Czech' both come down to us from the first ancient settlers of the land. 'Bohemia' is a derivation from the Boii tribe, a group of Celts who inhabited the western region of what is today the Czech Republic as early as 300 BC. Czechs themselves do not use the term though; they call the region Čechy, the word coming from the legend of a man named Čech who led his early Slavic followers Moses-like to the top of Říp Hill in north Bohemia.

As the words Bohemia and Czech both refer to the western part of the country, they should, in their strictest sense, only be associated with the inhabitants of this region. In the Czech language, it is a misnomer to call the entire country Čechy: the eastern region (approximately the eastern third, though the borders are vague) is known as Moravia (Morava) and its inhabitants as Moravians. The language is the same, but Moravians claim a slightly different culture based on the following distinctions: there was once a kingdom known as the

13

Great Moravian Empire, which ruled the area from the years AD 830—907; Moravia is geographically separated (loosely as it is) by the Bohemian–Moravian highlands; Moravians cling a bit more strongly to their folk traditions; and Moravians speak a more refined, polished, and textbook-precise Czech. The differences between Bohemians and Moravians are in fact so slight that you'll hardly notice them, though if you do have Moravian friends or colleagues, you'll impress them by being conscious of the distinction. It's 'politically correct' to refer to Prague as a Czech city and Brno as a Moravian one, but for practical purposes, it's all just called Czech.

Along the northern border with Poland lies the small area known as Silesia, again with a slightly different cultural heritage. Silesia and the Silesian people are a vague concept though, as there never was a Silesian state. The people are historically a mix of Poles, Germans, Czechs, and Moravians, inhabiting the region along the border and into southern Poland.

The very name of the country that is now the Czech Republic has changed several times over the course of its political development, and is still a source of confusion to some. This book occasionally uses the term 'the Czech lands' to represent the lands that the Czechs inhabit, that is, Bohemia, Moravia, and Silesia. Through most of this century the state of Czechoslovakia was a union of what are now the Czech and Slovak Republics; the two split amicably in 1993. This split was so peaceful, in fact, that it came to be known as the 'Velvet Divorce,' which is probably why many people outside the country still call it by its old name. Incidentally, when the separation occurred, there was some debate in the new government over what in fact the country should be named. The word Czech is an adjective, so it needed a substantive – Czechomoravia would have been a convenient and fair name, but then that would have left Silesia out, so they opted for the simplest solution.

Czechs don't like to be referred to as Eastern Europeans. Since the end of the Cold War, this division of Europe into two parts has become outdated. Historically the Czech lands have always been a key player in central Europe, literally a crossroads between the east and west, and this geographical position has always been an important factor in its own economic and cultural development. The 'West' is often referred to casually as western Europe and North America, though the changes going on now throughout the Czech Republic will soon render it as Western as any of these countries. So while it's an easy tag word to use, the sense of it is becoming less and less defined.

The population of the Czech Republic is 10.5 million, though there are several hundred thousand Czech nationals living in the US, Canada, and western Europe, countries to which Czechs emigrated throughout the 19th century, and to which they escaped during the Nazi and Soviet occupations. Centres of Czech culture have sprouted up in Chicago, Vancouver, rural Texas, parts of Australia, and even toward the east in Ukraine and Kazakhstan.

A BRIEF HISTORICAL BACKGROUND
We really have to go all the way back to the beginning of the Czech nation to properly understand the culture. Czechs hold a strong identity in their early ancestors, who ruled over long periods of peace and prosperity before and throughout the Middle Ages. The political story of the Czech lands from the 1500s to 1989 was almost exclusively one of non-independence, so today's Czechs take special pride in their past glory, and in their more recent successes at breaking the hold of foreign domination.

Czechs are a Slavic people, descendents of agrarian tribes who migrated to the region from the east around the 6th century BC. The early Slavs lived a peaceful existence, farming and living in close-knit communities, and initially adhering to pagan religious practices. By the 10th century the first Slavic royal line in the region, the Přemyslid dynasty, had emerged to rule what is now the Czech Republic and parts of Germany, Poland, and Slovakia.

From the time of the Přemysls and even before, Slavs were constantly intermingling with the Franks, a Germanic tribe with whom they alternately warred and traded. Most Czech towns that were founded between the 10th and 13th centuries had large numbers of German burghers; some cities, such as České Budějovice (Budweis), were almost entirely German.

The Přemysls were a mighty unifying force in the region, making peace with the Franks and converting the people to Christianity, an event which gave the kingdom membership status in the Holy Roman Empire. After the last Přemysl died in 1306, the kingdom was ruled by the House of Luxembourg, whose most prominent member was King Charles (Karel) IV. Although raised in France, Charles was half Bohemian, and he reigned over the nation's Golden Age, during which time Slavic farmers and Germanic tradesmen played equally integral roles in the development of the economy. Charles is by far the most revered of all Czech leaders. He served as not only their king, but also (concurrently) as Holy Roman Emperor, he gave Prague an outstanding architectural legacy, and he founded the first university in central Europe in 1348. Prague was one of the largest and most prosperous cities in Europe at this time.

The 1400s were a time of furious strife in all aspects of society, instigated by the attempted religious reforms of Jan Hus and the religious wars launched by his followers, the Hussites. Hus spoke out against the injustices of the established Catholic order; charges of heresy were laid upon him at the Council of Constance, and he was ultimately burned at the stake for refusing to recant, in 1415. Over the next two decades, a military wing of the Hussites terrorised the country, destroying all signs of Catholicism and wealth they could lay their hands on, and it wasn't until King Jiří of Poděbrady, a native Czech, was elected in 1458 that a measure of relative calm was attained. Jiří in fact was the ideological heir to the Přemysls and Luxembourgs, promoting international peace and security, though his reign was cut short by his early death, and the land was again plunged into political turmoil.

In 1526 the Hapsburgs were elected rulers of Bohemia and Moravia by the Czech nobility, bringing with them a whole slew of measures that would effectively stunt Czech intellectual growth for the next 300-plus years. The Hapsburgs consolidated power in 1620, when they quashed an uprising at the furious Battle of Bílá Hora (White Mountain). This was a momentous occasion in Czech and European history: Czech troops were trounced in a battle that launched the Thirty Years' War across the continent, and in a single day the fate of the nation was sealed until 1918. Catholicism was firmly reinstated as the counter-Reformation swept across much of Europe, German became the official language of most business endeavours, and all politics was dominated by decrees from Vienna (or from Hapsburg emperors living in Prague or elsewhere).

The mid-18th century saw the rebirth (some commentators in fact call it the birth) of Czech nationalism, commonly known as the National Revival. Writers and politicians such as František Palacký and composers such as Bedřich Smetana 'reawakened' a sense of national identity: the Czech language again became a source of national pride; Czech architecture came alive with several important projects, such as the National Theatre and the National Museum in Prague; and a movement towards independence developed with Tomáš Garrigue Masaryk's political work around the turn of the century.

Czechoslovakia

In 1918 Masaryk founded the independent state of Czechoslovakia. The idea to join the previously separate Czech and Slovak lands was conceived by Masaryk as a security measure, and was endorsed by US president Woodrow Wilson. For the first time in centuries, Czechs were ruled by their own leaders, placing full confidence in Masaryk and his cabinet, who functioned on a precept of social democracy, while enjoying economic prosperity. Masaryk remained in office until 1936, when his trusted foreign minister Edvard Beneš became president.

Masaryk's First Republic, as it is now called in perspective, was a mighty economic force; in fact, the state ranked eighth in the world in GDP per capita, largely due to German capital which made up three-fifths of the whole. The industrial and agricultural sectors were solid, and the country came to be famous especially for its engineering, automotive works, and military output.

Communism

All this was short-lived however. During World War II the country was entirely at the mercy of the Nazis. For three years after the War they were independent again under President Beneš, but with the Cold War getting underway, Czechs found themselves on the wrong side of the fence. Beneš was unable to quell the rising voice of the Communists, and, unable to form a coalition government, he instructed parliament to settle the matter on its own. Communist party members, who had been voted into office in 1946, thus won control of the government, and their leader, Klement Gottwald, became president in February 1948. The irony of it all is that the Communists were in fact freely elected.

By this time nearly all German and Austrian nationals living in the republic were transferred back to their homelands, even though their ancestors had lived here for generations. The forced expulsion of Germans from Sudetenland, or north Bohemia, is the source of an ongoing controversy in political ethics here.

The period from 1948 to 1989 was essentially a political blank. The politics of fear played by Communism had a dangerous effect on people's mentalities, and have instilled certain transitory mannerisms which will be discussed in subsequent parts of this book.

The Prague Spring uprising of 1968 was the lone hopeful event during this dark era, prompted by Party leader Alexander Dubček's calls for "socialism with a human face." Summer-long protests rallied behind Dubček's proposed reforms, though they ultimately resulted in a summons to Moscow, from whence Dubček returned a broken man. Soviet tanks occupied the city in August, and the rebellion was dismantled.

The spirit went underground, however, and a movement known as Charter 77 emerged to monitor political events, and its members, including the charismatic philosopher and playwright Václav Havel, became political prisoners themselves for their 'subversive' activities. The November–December 1989 revolution (termed the 'Velvet Revolution' for its remarkable lack of violence) was the pinnacle in a long buildup of frustrations, sparked into manifestation by the fall of the Berlin Wall in October. Massive strikes and civil disobedience finally brought about the resignation of the Communist officials, and free elections were held December 29th. Havel was elected president in a landslide, and a successful coalition government was formed.

Three years later the Slovak parliament elected to secede from Czechoslovak federation; this too was a peaceful event, and was hence dubbed the 'Velvet Divorce.' Since January 1, 1993, the Czech Republic has been a small, independent state with sights set firmly on integration with the European Union.

This memorial marks the scene of the Czechoslovak Revolution – often called the 'Velvet Revolution' for its lack of violent protest.

GOVERNMENT

For a nation that has had such a tumultuous political history, Czechs are surprisingly loathe to talk politics. Perhaps it's a hangover trait from Communism, when one was forbidden to debate or question the almighty Party directive. Perhaps it's because Czechs don't worry too much about anything beyond their personal comfort and contentedness. Or perhaps it's because the Czech Republic has had such a strong and able government since the revolution that any political discussion will only lead to general agreement with or indifference to the current events.

Czech politics today functions under a parliamentary democracy. Two hundred regional representatives are elected to the parliament, and the majority party elects its own leader, who serves as prime minister. There are currently thirteen political parties (one of which is a reformed Communist party), plus independents. The parliament is composed of sixteen ministries, such as those of agriculture, industry, finance, and justice, and numerous committees. General elections are held every four years for all legislative branch positions. A new senate was formed in November 1996, as a larger legislative body, its role is to provide more local representation.

One of the reasons for the Czech Republic's enormous success in the post-Communist era is its line of strong, clever politicians. Václav Klaus, representing the conservative Civic Democratic Party (ODS), became prime minister in 1992; before this he had served as minister of finance, and due to his keen grasp of the measures needed to transform a socialist economy to a market-based system, he has produced laudable accomplishments and has won praises both at home and abroad.

Klaus' seemingly firm position was shaken however, with the surprise results of the June 1996 elections. The prime minister's right wing ODS party won the most votes, with 29.6% but with much stronger competition from the left wing Social Democrats (ČSSD), who garnered an unexpected 26.4%, the three-party coalition he headed lost its majority in the parliament by a mere two seats. After a month of scrambling to form a new government, Klaus maintained his position as prime minister and the coalition, composed of the similar-minded ODS, ODA (Civic Democratic Alliance) and KDU-ČSL (Christian Democratic Union–Czech People's Party), retained control over all sixteen ministries, The suddenly popular Miloš Zeman, leader of the Social Democrats, became chairman of the parliament, a position which gives him leverage in what should be increasingly fragmented parliamentary debate throughout the term of government.

Klaus and the ruling coalition had been fully expected to continue on their merry way until the year 2000 but a weak advertising campaign, combined with a low voter turnout (largely over-confident ODS voters who stayed at home) brought the left wingers back into the fray. Rural and lower income voters, tired of living in a strange

21

new world of high taxation, inflation and competition on a scale previously unknown, turned out in hope of slowing down the privatisation machine when it affected issues such as the cost of housing and transportation. Despite the turmoil it isn't nearly as volatile as in neighbouring countries such as Hungary, Poland and Slovakia, who have elected former Communist officials back into power. The Communist and extreme right wing parties did make gains in the 1996 elections but they remain insignificant. Given Klaus' notoriously self-assured and uncompromising style, Czech politics should continue roughly as it has in the recent past.

The Role of the President

Standing aside from the parliament is the president. The president is not a member of parliament, though he is voted into power by the parliament. His job is largely symbolic and as figurehead of the nation, he usually represents the Czech Republic at international functions. The real job of running the country, however, lies in the hands of the prime minister.

Václav Havel stepped down as president in mid-1992 in protest of the forthcoming secession of Slovakia, claiming he didn't want to preside over the breakup of a state. He was then reelected president of the Czech Republic in February 1993, and looks a sure bet to win reelection for as long as he runs. Havel has been noted by some as being the incarnation of the Greek's 'philosopher king,' a label which he humbly denies, especially as he has little executive power anyway. Nevertheless, it is tempting to see him in the light of great Czech leaders, from the Přemysls to King Charles IV to Masaryk.

Of course the country faces enormous difficulties, as the job of overhauling a period of nearly 50 years of social and economic stagnation is a gargantuan undertaking. The top issue on all agendas is strengthening the economy, and many Czechs are oblivious to all else.

THE ECONOMY

The Czechs have historically been a wealthy nation; in fact, the goal now seems to be to regain the level of prosperity the state enjoyed up to the time of the Nazi and Communist takeovers. The socially planned economy ruined all market orientations, though Czechs are rapidly reasserting their will to succeed.

HISTORIC ECONOMIC LEVEL ←———

The Communist Legacy

Immediately after the Communist takeover in 1948, most private property and privately owned companies were nationalised. What this essentially meant was that private citizens lost ownership of their homes and businesses, and job descriptions changed as everything was ruled from the top down. Market economy fundamentals such as supply and demand were suddenly irrelevant, as farms and factories were geared for production, with little relation to consumerism. And to propound the pride of the working class, the central authority forced drastic measures, such as employing certain intellectuals as window washers and food canners.

There was no need for specialisation, and therefore machinery works turned out the same models year after year, with the intention only of meeting quotas – this is why most of the trains you see look like they've been running since the 1940s. Shops had all the basic goods, but there was very little choice involved in purchasing them: you took what was offered. Prices and salaries remained almost unchanged for decades; though both are rising steadily now, this is why so many domestic products are still cheap by Western standards.

The concept of service was damaged as well. Where the individual was merely a functioning cell in the organism, and few were satisfied with their menial jobs, life became a monotonous existence. The service industry was reduced to its bare bones – this is why many hotels, restaurants, and government offices are still staffed with inattentive and surly employees.

Post–1989: The Shift to the Market Economy

Extraordinary changes have taken place since 1989. The Czech economy is far and away the healthiest of the former East Bloc, due to the strong measures taken initially by the fiscally conservative government of Václav Klaus.

The term 'shock therapy' has been applied often and aptly to the new economic policies. Fundamental changes were imposed immediately, though where neighbouring countries such as Slovakia and Hungary have sputtered along, changing tactics when problems arose, the Czech Republic has taken measured risks and pushed forward. Of course, shock therapy also meant shock to the people, who suddenly faced unprecedented inflation and vastly different job requirements. Klaus has done an admirable job of strictly monitoring the transformation, easing the pain by continuing government assistance to essential enterprises such as transportation, housing, and health care.

Inflation has held steady since the initial 100% figure of 1990; in 1994 it was 10%, and each year since it has dipped down nearly a whole percentage point – in 1996 it stood at 8.2 %. Salaries, however, have not kept pace. The national average wage in 1995 was approximately US$350 a month – enough for subsistence living, but precious little else. Somehow the national average is not a fair indicator though: many Czechs involved in private business are earning US$2000 a month and more, which places them in the highest tax bracket, and renders a 25 cent beer laughably cheap.

Amazingly, unemployment has remained very low, at around 3% nationwide. The figure in Prague is less than 1%, making the city a world of opportunity for those seeking work and advancement.

GDP is growing steadily and the currency remains strong and stable. Yet the Czech Republic faced a trade deficit of US$3.8 billion in 1995: while the country has the advantage of low labour costs and a strong history of manufacturing, imports continue to flow in with ever increasing public demand. Industrial strength is based in heavy machinery, transportation equipment, chemicals, and food production. Tourism is now a huge source of income as well. Chief agricultural products include potatoes, wheat, barley, hops, and sugar beets.

Privatisation

The most important step taken in 1991 (after a year's worth of preparation) was that of privatisation of property owned by the government. Everything from factories to farms to homes to businesses had been nationalised by the Communists in 1948, and the process of returning property to the original owners, and of selling off other holdings, has been long and complicated. A system of restitution was established whereby persons who owned property previous to 1948 were eligible to reclaim it, though this has encountered predictable squabbles over ownership rights. Germans who had been kicked out in 1946 often laid claim to real estate subsequently taken over by Czechs, and some Jews had claims of their own dating back to pre-Nazi 1938.

Property that was not subject to restitution was sold through a unique system of privatisation vouchers. All Czech citizens over age 18 were allotted a book of vouchers which they could use to invest in whatever company they chose on the market. The Prague Stock Exchange reopened in 1993, and by the end of 1996 over 90% of formerly state-owned firms were in private hands.

Enormous amounts of foreign investment money have greatly aided the transformation. Prague is the base of hundreds of foreign

25

companies expanding their operations not only in the Czech Republic, but throughout central and eastern Europe. (Who, indeed, would choose to live anywhere else if the business can be managed in Prague?) The local workforce is highly skilled and labour costs are much lower than in neighbouring west European countries. The budget runs on a surplus and foreign debt is low; in short, the Czech Republic has all the right ingredients for prosperity. Czech financial experts no longer refer to the economy as 'emerging' – it has already emerged. The rewards for this are evident in the Czech Republic's new membership in the Organization for Economic Cooperation and Development (OECD), and its concrete hope to join the European Union by 2000.

RELIGION

Czechs overall are not a religious people, which is surprising considering the country's large number of churches and its proximity to such heavily Catholic countries such as Poland and Slovakia. Perhaps again this can be traced through history.

The early Slavs were pagan, though the Přemysls Christianised them with help from the Byzantine missionaries Cyril and Methodius in 863. Catholicism reigned throughout Europe during the Middle Ages, but by the beginning of the 15th century, voices in Bohemia led the cry for reform. The work of Jan Hus was instrumental in the development of Protestantism: a few decades after his execution Martin Luther emerged to organise the first true Protestant faith in Europe. Although the strong winds of the counter-Reformation blew through the Czech lands with especial force, the people were reluctant to re-adopt Catholicism. Under Communism, religion was effectively banned. Priests and monks were forcibly removed from office, and churchgoers worshipped at their own risk.

Judaism was firmly established as early as the 10th century, and Prague especially was home to a large Jewish population up until the Nazi invasion. The Josefov district of Prague's Old Town was

Art Nouveau in Prague's Jewish Quarter.

inhabited by several thousand Jews until the end of the last century, when the ghetto was demolished for urban renewal. Jews suffered the same persecutions in the Czech lands as everywhere, and by the end of World War II, nearly 80,000 Czech Jews had been exterminated in Nazi concentration camps. Only a handful remain today.

Those Czechs that do worship today are predominantly Catholic, but the number of active believers is remarkably low. Most churches have less than full capacity services, and the majority of worshippers are the elderly. Why?

Czechs are somewhat agnostic, preferring independent thought and their own folk traditions. Most people will quite openly and without hesitation state, for example, that there is no God, and when we die, we simply lie underground, end of story. Czechs are in this sense true sceptics, not only in religious matters but in their general social outlook.

27

Given their history of religious and political oppression, one can admire the wit and clarity of the response to any institutionalisation or organisation. Bitter and pessimistic they are not; straightforward, upbeat, and well-rooted in their normal life, they are a sensible people.

FALLOUT FROM COMMUNISM

The damage done by Communism has already been mentioned. Through these comments, and those in subsequent parts of this book, it should become clear that Communism was a real leech that Czechs are still working to disengage from; this is a long term, ongoing project.

It is impossible for any of us who did not live under this system to really imagine what it was like. Controls were extremely tight – speech and expression were censored, professionals risked their careers (and in extreme cases, their children's too) if they didn't join the Party, and these measures had remarkable effects on peoples' ways of thinking. Most everybody detested (but silently accepted) the system they were in, though with such oppressive societal monitoring, the effect was of the beaten dog who simply gives in and endures the whipping. The weight of it all pressed down and produced a lifeless person. In a system which successfully stamped out individuality, people lost their sense of purpose and importance, and hence, incentive.

I cannot give an accurate account of real life under this system, I can only relay the effects and changes since then. Virtually everything that is covered in this book has been touched in negative ways by Communism, which I've tried to work in where appropriate, so please be aware that many of the social and business traits discussed below have been tainted by the system, from which it will still take years to completely disentangle, yet changes are taking place at a remarkable rate, such that in time many of these comments will become obsolete.

For a better idea of what life was like here under this regime, refer directly to contemporary writers such as Václav Havel, Ivan Klíma, and Josef Škvorecký, whose works are mentioned at the back of this book.

PRAGUE LORE: FOLK TALES AND SEMI-TRUTHS

The legends swirling about Prague are older than the city itself. Many of course are purely fairy tales, though they have a special power that the natives respect. Some have elements of truth in them, or emerge from true scenarios and events, and some are historically documented facts, odd and intriguing enough to merit mention.

The origin of the city is a legend in itself. Around the 7th century or so, Libuše was princess of the Slavs who settled on the hill at Vyšehrad, and whose social structure was largely governed by women. She is said to have foreseen a great city rising from the opposite banks, whose glory would "touch the stars." A couple of centuries later, Hradčany became the seat of the first Přemyslid dynasty in the Bohemian lands.

Vyšehrad was also an important Přemyslid stronghold, which included at one time a prison. A Bohemian prince, Horymír, was sentenced to death here, though was mistakenly granted a last request: to ride his horse one last time around the castle grounds. The horse knew what to do and leapt the wall, sliding down the cliff to the Vltava, where his rider swam away to freedom.

Sometime around the Přemyslid era, a great Bohemian warrior and traveller named Bruncvík wandered the earth with his lion and magic sword, now supposedly buried in Charles Bridge. Upon moments of great national danger, prince Václav, the patron saint, will grab up the sword and shout "heads off!" and all the nation's enemies will disappear.

Prague's streets are littered with monsters and ghosts, the most famous of which is the Golem. A creation of Rabbi Löwe, who in fact was the chief rabbi of the Jewish Quarter in the 16th century, this brute was brought to life by a piece of donkey skin which Rabbi Löwe placed under his tongue (modern interpretation has the Golem's soft spot in his forehead). As all man-made beings, though, the Golem started to become dangerous and uncontrollable, wreaking havoc

The Golem – fairy tale monster of Prague's Jewish Quarter; today he lends his name to a film festival.

throughout the quarter until his master was forced to destroy the donkey skin pergamen and bury the Golem in the attic of the Old New Synagogue.

Several lesser critters of the Old Town include the stone knight of Platnéřská Street, who killed the local blacksmith's daughter after she refused his love. He then turned to iron and returns once every 100 years to find her – though nobody knows when the last visit was. The Karolinum is haunted by the ghost of an exceedingly tall man who sold his corpse to Charles University for the benefit of science – he now begs money from tourists to buy back his skeleton. Several of

Prague's pubs are haunted by the *vodník*, a little man in an overcoat who lives under Charles Bridge, wooing little girls into his lair. He can be detected by the pool of water under his pub seat. The ghost of a merchant Turk and his former lover lurk around the Hotel Ungelt, where he killed her in a romantic fury – the headless body of the girl supposedly lies in the basement.

Unfortunately true is the character of Mydlář the Axeman, who is responsible for the beheadings of 24 Bohemian noblemen on 21 June 1621 as a Hapsburg punishment to the instigators of the uprising that ended in defeat at Bílá Hora. Perhaps the rebels were asking for it though; three years earlier they had thrown two of the ruling governors out the window of the Ludvík Wing at Prague Castle in the second defenestration of Prague. The first defenestration was a similarly rebellious bloody effort by the Hussites, who did the same from the New Town Hall on Karlovo náměstí in 1420.

Medieval Old Town Prague suffered numerous floods over its first few centuries, finally prompting the residents to raise the street level several metres. This contributed to the rich Gothic make-up of the city, though much of the Old Town's ancient foundations are now buried underground.

During the reign of Rudolf II the city was a European cultural centre, with one of Europe's richest collections of fine art (which was subsequently pilfered by the Swedes during the Thirty Years' War). Rudolf also surrounded himself with astronomers, astrologers, and alchemists – he was more intent on exploring the heavens and turning lead into gold than in ruling the Austrian empire. Results were mixed; while Edward Kelly never managed to turn lead into anything but molten lead, astronomers Tycho de Brahe and Johannes Kepler made significant advances in our knowledge of the heavens.

On a more mundane level, chimney sweepers *(komínicí)* are to this day considered a lucky charm. Though the practice is dying, it is still a sign of luck if a coal-dusted chimney sweep brushes against you; even more rewarding is to rub the button on his lapel.

— *Chapter Two* —

CZECH CHARACTERISTICS

THE CZECH IDENTITY

One tends to generalise about a people when one becomes familiar with them. While it is senseless and even dangerous to group people into categories, it's inevitable, and for our purposes, it is important to understand character traits and mannerisms. Recognising these is a step towards better cultural awareness, which means better appreciation of the time spent in that society. The Czechs are a very small and homogenous nation, and anyone who has spent any amount of time amongst them can quite easily come up with a few constituent features. Some of these will hit you in the face; some are more subtle and it takes quite a bit of probing to start to discern patterns.

Digging into the source of these traits is a revealing exercise. Robert B. Pynsent's excellent book, *Questions of Identity: Czech and Slovak Ideas of Nationality and Personality,* serves as a source and support for many of the following observations. In it he speaks of the 'question' of identity being a study of a nation's history, language, and cultural development. Czechs have a very definite identity, based in their own ethnic roots and historical mingling with other nations – it is thus a curious blend of cultures and ideologies. The years under Communism had an additional lasting (and destructive) effect on the character of the people – so many of the traits discussed below are in effect transitive, and difficult to pinpoint. It's amazing, in fact, to see how influential politics can be on society in this regard.

So let's speak of some of these, with full respect to the fact that what follows is a broad scope of generalisations, certainly not to be applied to all Czechs in all situations, and that the negative ones will only bother you if you let them.

Czechs as Slavic, Czechs as Germanic

While Czechs ethnically are Slavs, we can see from the very dawn of their nationhood that the course of events through their entire history is intrinsically interwoven with Germans and German-speaking Austrians. A well respected Czech intellectual of the early 20th century, Josef Pekař, observes that both Czechs and Germans have a legitimate home in Bohemia, and he even goes so far as to say that the Czechs' economic and cultural success is a direct result of German education. If one considers that the Hapsburgs ruled the Czech lands from the age of the late Renaissance through the Baroque and Romantic eras into the 20th century, it can be seen that huge cultural advances were made during this long era, even though it was not particularly within a Czech framework. This, indeed, is Pekař's point: that cultural development in the Czech lands was a cosmopolitan, European endeavour.

Most agree that Czechs are much less 'Slavic' than their neighbours – the simple fact of geography certainly contributes to this idea (the Czech Republic is the westernmost Slavic country, bordering Germany and Austria). Czechs themselves, meanwhile, hold a strong aversion to anything German, and the very idea of insinuating their 'Germanness' is taken as quite an insult.

The Bridge Metaphor

Czechs seem to believe that they occupy a special place in the world, or at least they occupy a central role in Europe, and this latter is a valid precept. They feel themselves to be a sort of bridge between east and west: the east, which happens to be only now emerging from Communism, and incidentally is predominantly Slavic; and the west, which has long been more culturally open and economically "free," and is at least in part Germanic. But, it must be noted, a bridge connects points A and B without really belonging to either; Czechs in this way defy classification.

The Quiet Nature

Your first impression of Czechs will likely be that they are a cold and reserved people, and this could well be your single greatest barrier in adjusting to the culture. Outwardly, this is not an exuberant nation: Czechs aren't given to emotional displays, and interaction with strangers – in shops, on the metro – are generally kept to impersonal comments and curt replies, if anything at all. Part of this attitude may stem from the simple fact that they live in a climate which is cold and dark for half the year.

There are of course vast differences between the attitudes of those living in the city and those in the countryside. Prague can feel like a nasty city at times, especially in the heart of winter when nobody's happy; meanwhile you'll find residents of small towns and villages more friendly and open.

The Czech sense of community and friendship is a little more protected and sheltered than that of many countries. Czechs have a strong sense of privacy, and of the closeness of the family unit. They tend to stay at home, and don't really venture out except to go to the pub or the cottage; life on the street, as practised in most Asian and Mediterranean countries, for example, does not take place here.

Another factor in this behaviour is quite likely the lingering effects of Communist societal monitoring. A sense of insecurity and distrust was implanted in the citizens, who lived in dull fear of being observed or judged. Václav Havel, in his essay "Article 202" from the collection *Open Letters*, writes of this "power that is happiest when people don't socialise too much with each other (that is, unless the authorities organise and control it themselves), when they don't go out very often and, when they do go out, always behave with proper humility. It's a power that finds it convenient when people keep an eye on each other, watch each other, are afraid of each other, a power that sees society as an obedient herd whose duty is to be permanently grateful that it has what it has." In such a herd mentality, where the individual has no responsibility to himself or others, he accepts impersonality. This likely reinforced the Czech tendency to self-sufficiency and as a defence mechanism, they have learned how to take care of themselves.

Don't expect, upon moving into your new home, to be welcomed by your neighbours, or even to be greeted in a friendly way the first few times they see you. In fact, don't expect to get to know your neighbours at all. Most apartments in Prague and around the country have been lived in by the same families for years, and they start to get suspicious when there is some sort of change.

Surprisingly, they don't put too much effort into getting to know one another. I lived for nearly three years in an apartment in Prague and only very rarely saw my neighbours, never once exchanging anything more than a quiet *dobrý den*. If this happens to you, and it probably will, don't take it as a snub: it's just how it is. It is interesting to note, meanwhile, that Czechs think of themselves as naturally warm and friendly, though it does take time to dig into this deep-rooted layer of hospitality.

Czechs are often shy and quiet when meeting people for the first time. Though they are firm in their beliefs and they do enjoy a good conversation, they are sometimes wary of speaking out. Czechs in their day to day lives are simply a calm and reserved people, and they admire modesty and humility in all situations. If you keep a low profile and approach Czechs with a minimum of crassness and vanity, you'll make a positive impression.

The tone of voice used in conversations is always level, rarely raising into a shout. Czechs in fact complain about Germans and Americans especially for speaking so loudly, confidently, and forcefully.

You could go so far as to say that Czechs are a passive people. It seems they focus on what they are doing with their own lives, and they try to ignore any perceived disturbances therein. Problematic situations often end up in embarrassed silences and looks of "Oh, I just wish this would go away." A friend of mine, who is American, relates the story of how she once fell as she was boarding a bus; her bags went flying and she ended up on her knees. Nobody made any effort to help – her fellow passengers just watched, or turned away, embarrassed. So she bravely got up and announced, in Czech, "Thanks, it's OK, I'm fine!" The humour was lost on them.

Don't let this intimidate you, though and don't make the mistake of making negative generalisations about your host people. It's easy to have something like this happen and instantly criticise Czechs for being so this-and-that, but this is just a symptom of the down period of culture shock. You're just as likely to witness the encouraging sight of a passenger giving up his seat to a senior citizen.

Judging from the glum faces you see on the metro, and the grey clothes and withdrawn mannerisms you first encounter, your first image may be of a certain detachedness on the part of Czechs, even of non-interest in the world around. It does take an effort to get beyond this. While it is easy to grumble about the rude service at the newsagents, the gruff attitude of the waiters, and the seeming non-response of Czechs to events around them, a little probing into their casual lifestyle reveals a wealth of spirit and life.

Merriness and Drinking
Czech merriness is a dearly held trait, though it is usually experienced in private, after a bond of friendship and trust has been established.

Though Czechs rarely entertain at home, social gatherings often quickly turn into light-hearted joking, aided in part by the national passion for drink.

Most drinking is done in the pub in the evenings, though there is always an excuse to lubricate. Birthdays and name-days *(svátky)* often turn into noontime office parties, and friendship is celebrated in many different guises over a beer or two.

I recall one evening I was suffering from a cold, so the students in my English class volunteered to end the lesson early. I was on very friendly terms with them, and one of them invited me up to his flat for 'a drink' – home-made *slivovice* (plum brandy), supposedly the best cure for minor ailments. One drink of course became several and each time I looked at my glass it was full. I ended up stumbling home three hours later. At the next lesson the culprit looked at me with a sly grin: "So the sore throat is gone? But you woke up with a headache."

No, they are not a nation of alcoholics. Czechs drink in a very social way, for camaraderie, for fun, and they do moderate, though

For Czechs, socialising and drinking often go hand in hand.

their levels of moderation are significantly higher than most. Polls show that Czechs are far and away the greatest consumers of beer per capita, well above neighbouring guzzlers Germany and Belgium.

When questioned about their love and capacity for drink, Czechs always put it into perspective. Reports from places such as Russia indicate a wild abandon in many circles, excesses that Czechs look down upon. Drinking is a social event, one with its own standards of refinement. Czechs abstain in formal situations – at business lunches they often order just mineral water or coffee, and if they are driving they strictly avoid alcohol. Drinking is reserved for certain situations, but when those times come up, they like to let loose.

Czech Folk

Czechs retain a strong folk element. All Czech homes are decorated with lace curtains and handicrafts, and they treasure their record and photo collections, books on art and culture, and family heirlooms. Markets around the country, even in the touristy areas of Prague, are full of trinkets such as wooden toys and Bohemian crystal. Moravians especially take a very casual approach to life, and folk music and craft festivals abound in the summer. Czechs love the simple life found in nature, and they escape whenever possible to their cottages in the country.

The love of nature is deeply-rooted trait. Slavs have traditionally been farmers, and therefore have developed a strong appreciation of and love for nature. Pynsent notes the work of Johann Gottfried von Herder, a German writer of the last century who speaks of Slavs historically occupying unclaimed land, often wasteland, tilling it, and building functioning communities. Furthermore, they rarely fought over land, achieving peaceful settlements through diplomatic means.

There is a Czech saying which goes: "Every man must build a house, plant a tree, and raise children." A friend of mine's father took the proverb to heart: he built a country cottage entirely on his own, even refusing offers of help from friends and family, and this for him was a humble, though significant, expression of freedom (a particularly meaningful one under the former regime). The work doesn't stop there though; he, like so many Czechs, takes great pride in the upkeep of the cottage, and he and his wife maintain a large garden producing apples, pears, garlic, and carrots.

Every weekend in the summer is spent out in the country, and should you be lucky enough to become well acquainted with a Czech friend, you'll find a visit to their cottage one of the most rewarding experiences of your stay. Czechs take their country escapes very seriously, finding peace and relaxation in returning to the woods. Evenings are often spent in front of a campfire, where family and friends gather for conversation, song, and beer.

Czech Non-Conformity

Perhaps it is an escape mentality which plays in here. Czech lore is filled with the nonconformist, escape-minded mentality which exhibits itself in such weekend activity. To call Czechs nonconformist is not to say rebellious or temperamental, however; it is a quietly defensive trait developed through history. While the nation bristled under foreign occupation for so many centuries, the people found comfort in their country roots.

Czechs take an intellectual pride in their informed separatism. Jan Hus set the ball rolling with his challenge to the Church, and Czechs were reluctant members of the Hapsburg Empire for nearly four hundred years. Novelist Jaroslav Hašek made his mark on the Czech literary world by introducing the playfully deviant personage of Soldier Schweik in his World War I-era book *The Good Soldier Schweik*. The Schweik character is an embodiment of a particular element in the Czech spirit, which Czechs today freely admit as a valid stereotype. Schweik is an unwilling Czech soldier in the Austrian army, a happy-go-lucky swiller of good beer with an uncanny ability to make a hash of any situation, and emerge the unwitting victor. Society all around is restrictive, controlling, pressing, yet nothing seems to faze Schweik. His light-hearted approach to resolving sticky situations is a characteristic that endears him to the reader and demonstrates a particular Czech tendency to make light of difficulty and to find a way around it.

Pohoda: The Life of Ease

Czechs pride themselves on knowing the priorities in life – family, wellbeing, and an appreciation of the simple things in life. There is a very descriptive word, *pohoda*, which means something like comfort, ease, or wellbeing; its root is similar to that of the words for value, worth, or goodness, and it is used in many situations to say that everything is as it should be.

The Well Rounded Czech

As they say, *Češi umí* – Czechs know how. It's that simple. You will soon realise in most any conversation with a Czech that they are well educated and appreciative of culture; in fact this is an excellent topic of conversation in virtually any situation, and you may well find yourself and your country the subject of a lively discussion. While Czechs are quite a homogenous people, they have cosmopolitan interests.

Czech primary and secondary schools are excellent, and students seem to retain much of what they are taught. Their position in the heart of Europe undoubtedly instills an awareness of the world around – not only do Czechs know every last detail of their own country, they are surprisingly knowledgeable of many aspects of European culture in general. In fact, one common perception that Czechs have about Americans is that they are not educated, that they are unlearned in languages and the arts, which of course are an essential component of European life.

The Musical Inclination

Co Čech, to musikant (Every Czech is a musician): all Czechs are well-acquainted with music, everything from folk songs to classical music.

Folk songs, especially *trempink* (tramping) songs are known and loved by all. Evenings in local pubs may witness an accordion player striking up a tune, and soon the table of beer-toting old ladies and grizzled men starts to mumble out the classic old lines, covering themes such as laying out in a tent under the stars, or running off to the woods with your best friend's girl. The tempo picks up with a few more drinks, and soon the whole room is misty-eyed and laughing along with it all.

Even the young, while raised (in the past six years at least) on rock 'n' roll, are wont to pull out guitars and sing the old traditionals, some of which take on an international flavour: Bob Dylan is widely known, and one of the most popular folk songs is John Denver's "Country Roads," sung in Czech.

Music has a special power to inspire, and under Communism the influences of American and British rock music played an instrumental role in the development of political awareness. The Beatles were

Dixieland in December. Jazz musicians in Prague's Old Town Square.

41

virtually banned during the 60s, 70s, and 80s, though the message was widely distributed through underground outlets. The John Lennon Wall in Prague was, and still is, a gathering place for Czech youth's quiet counter-culture. Somehow the wall survived the final decade of Communist rule intact, via numerous midnight repaintings. In the 1970s, an underground Prague band called Plastic People of the Universe was censored by the authorities; this act was the first in a series of protests by Charter 77, a political watchdog which was formed to monitor human rights violations under the auspices of the Helsinki Accords.

Czech children all are encouraged to pick up an instrument; it's considered part of the development of the mind. Similarly, children are all taught how to dance properly. As winter balls are an important event in the social calendar, it is important to know how to waltz and polka.

Linguistic Sensibility

Again, Czechs have a fitting expression: *Kolik jazyků znáš, tolikrát jsi člověkem.* (You are as many people as the number of languages you know.)

Most educated Czechs speak two or three languages; those who do not speak English or German are working at it now. Of course, under the entire Hapsburg reign, many Czechs spoke German out of necessity. Older Czechs especially speak German: it was in their lifetime that the country was ruled by German-speakers, whether Hapsburg or Nazi. Under Communism, all schoolchildren were forced to learn Russian, which everyone is now doing their honest best to forget. The sophistiqué speak French, and it's interesting to note the haute-culture affinities that the French and Czechs have for one another. English is now the language of preference. Just after the 1989 revolution, language schools were flooded with students, and by now almost anyone in university or business speaks at least some English.

Love of the Czech language was a key to the National Revival of the nineteenth century. Writers such as František Palacký and Josef

Jungmann contributed enormously to national sensitivity through their works on the question of Czech identity and history. Reverence is paid to Jan Hus, who, as rector of the Charles University, developed a precise system of spelling and pronunciation which is still followed today. The very name of the Přemyslid dynasty implies a certain incisiveness: the word is almost identical to the verb *přemyslet* (to think about).

Czechs express a sincere appreciation for foreigners who learn to speak their language. While acknowledging that it is extremely difficult to master, and that it is insignificant outside their tiny country, they revel in its beauty, and have deep respect for anyone who is 'sympathetic' enough to learn it.

Human Diplomacy

Such intellectual versatility, as one Slovak philosopher calls it, certainly contributes to a universal love for peace and democracy. The medieval kingdoms functioned on a basis of international trade and relative economic freedom. Bohemia has always been made up of cohabiting Czechs and Germans, and Jews maintained a strong presence from the 10th century straight through till World War II. Masaryk's achievement of an independent Czechoslovakia in 1918 was a great triumph, in which the long sought dream of an independent, democratic state for the Czech people was finally attained.

It's interesting to note that the Velvet Revolution of 1989 was conducted purely on the basis of civil disobedience, with a complete lack of violence on the part of the protesters. And when the Czech Republic and Slovakia split in 1993, the event was simply a political decision, in which the citizens raised only a curious voice. Compare these two peaceful events with similar happenings in Romania and the former Yugoslavia, respectively.

Several commentators note that this peaceful nature hasn't always worked to the Czechs' benefit. In fact, at times it may have contributed to their undoing. Not that they didn't fight when called upon to do so:

43

the Hussites were ferocious warriors against Catholicism; Czech soldiers fought bravely, but were simply overpowered in the Battle of Bílá Hora; and the number of plaques you see on buildings in Prague commemorating the victims of the Prague Uprising of May 1945 attests to the will of the people to destroy Nazism. Yet Czech pride and nationalism is kept within an intellectual sphere. They may distrust and disapprove and be disdainful of outsiders, but their peaceful nature precludes confrontation: they would often just prefer to look away and ignore a trouble spot, even taking on a self-defeating 'there's nothing I can do' attitude.

Motionlessness

Herder comments on what he calls the Czechs' submissiveness and obedience. Arnošt Procházka, a Czech contemporary of his, even goes so far as to declare: "We are shallow and flabby. We love feebleness; we take pleasure in torpor; we protect and tend our feebleness and torpor like flowers in a greenhouse." And as this passage indicates, Czechs are quite good at complaining. They seem comfortable sympathising with how difficult things are – it just comes naturally to shake the head in disgust and mutter, "Oh it's terrible."

You come across the words 'problem' and 'normal' a lot. Anything which is not quite within the realm of 'normality' is difficult to grasp, and therefore creates a 'problem.' The irony, though, is that not only are they accustomed to saying that something is a problem, they seem to have little initiative to change it. Why make something easy? They are apt to joke. Meanwhile, they are sometimes content to just let things happen as they will – perhaps this is a reasonable acceptance of life as it is.

Communism seems to have exacerbated the tendency to mope. In one of his first speeches after taking over the presidency in December 1989, Václav Havel warned about the learned incapacity to think, which Communism instilled and which Czechs are now trying to shake. Many of the 'negative' traits spoken of here are instantly and categorically put down by Czechs as a result of the mindset of Communism. One Czech friend, for example, concurs with the trait, that so many people spend so much time complaining about 'problems' without offering any solutions, and accepting the notion that this is their lot. Yet she falls into her own trap, shaking her head and turning up her nose: "It was terrible! And now we don't know what to do about it."

Self Pity

The Czechs have spent many centuries under foreign rule, so it's understandable that they would adopt an attitude of self-pity. Many observers refer to the defeat at the Battle of Bílá Hora as the 'fall' of the Czech nation. Similarly, the internationally known novelist Milan Kundera laments 'the Czech lot' in one of his works.

Perhaps this attitude helps explain the abundance of martyrs in Czech history, through which Czechs may form a self identification. First and foremost among these is sv. Václav (St. Wenceslas), the patron saint of the nation. Václav was a Přemyslid prince who founded the first cathedral at Prague Castle, and who was murdered by his own brother, Boleslav the Cruel. With equally great aplomb, Jan Hus's martyrdom was a rallying cry for his followers, who still exist today, at least in the name of the Hussite church. And in more recent times, Jan Palach was an 18-year-old student who set himself on fire in protest of the Soviet invasion of 1968. Each of these occupies a special point of reverence in the Czech psyche.

Pragmatism

Nonetheless, Czechs are a practical people. Once you get past the vagaries of certain business practices and stagnant personalities, they are inherently logical, practical, and efficient. Part of the reason for the country's great economic success of late is the unrelenting drive of its citizens to better their lives, and so they are working harder than ever. Hard work means material reward, and this is the goal of virtually every Czech you are bound to meet – indeed, this allows the life of ease that everyone wants.

Czechs have an inbuilt sense of order and classification: almost every aspect of life is placed in neat little cubes. They generally live in small apartments, they follow a daily pattern of work, rest, and sleep, and the life cycle is remarkable for its predictability. They also organise their thought process and world view into compact functional units and they tend to draw up focused ideas and opinions. They will often launch into explanations of things they may know nothing about, and they may categorise people and situations, often with no regard for 'political correctness' which Americans and others take so seriously. Again, such opinions are characteristic of a particular way of organising the world, and Czechs tend to cling rather stubbornly to these.

Humour

You will eventually begin to notice a deep-rooted sarcasm, perhaps a necessary outgrowth of any small nation's pride. Czechs have a subtle and dry sense of humour, and they seem to take everything life throws at them with a grain of salt. One joke that emerged from the Communist era is very telling: regarding the exhortations to work, to build a socialist society, Czechs retorted, "We pretend to work and they pretend to pay us." I once saw a statue erected during the Communist era, decorated with the hammer and sickle and "Dedicated to the victims of war and oppression, 1914—1918 and 1938—1945." Underneath, someone had added a plaque with the telling dates "1948—1989." Of course the humour isn't limited to the oppressors from the East: with so many Americans in Prague now, the locals have adopted a sort of 'Oh, you again' attitude. A cartoon in a Czech newspaper thus referred to the 1995 space hook-up of American and Russian astronauts, with a woman querying her husband, "The Americans and Russians together in space? Finally! Does that mean all of them?"

The Sum Of It All: Czech Pride

Through all these generalisations, one can see a strong, deeply rooted national pride. Having lived through several centuries of foreign occupation, Czechs are stubbornly, almost defensively proud, and yet they approach the world today with an admirably fresh, youthful face. Perhaps it's fitting that the symbol on the national seal is the lion.

One simple event sums it up for me. During an English course for intermediate level adults, I posed one student the conversation topic question, "Of what are you proud?" I expected an answer relating to his entrepreneurial success, or the fact that his son is a university student, but he just shrugged his shoulders and looked at me as if it were a silly question: "I am proud that I am Czech."

CZECH IMPRESSIONS OF OTHERS

Czechs overall are extremely curious about foreign culture, and it's surprising what they are apt to know. Yet they still have had relatively little direct contact with other nationalities, so there can be many misunderstandings.

Americans are held in high regard here, undoubtedly because they were the 'enemy' for so many years. Many Czechs are insatiably curious about American pop culture, cars, military strength, and wealth, though those who have encountered Americans personally or have visited the US may have their reservations. Americans are seen as being strong and productive, direct, knowing what they want and being able to achieve it, though American confidence and the smiley all-is-well mentality is seen as superficial. Americans are thought of as a bit uncultured when it comes to European history and society, so it makes a great impression if you are an American and direct your behaviour towards humility and a genuine interest in the local people.

If you're German, you may be the object of a light scorn for all the damage your country did to the Czechs during World War II. Germans have an image of being loud and demanding – which disturbs the local peace. Again, approach the locals with humility and a desire to know and understand them.

Most other European nationals are still quite unknown to most Czechs, and therefore they have no real impression, positive or negative, of them. The British are generally seen as being cold, Italians as being fashionable and enthusiastic, and the French as being highly cultivated, though real knowledge of other cultures is limited. Czechs are always curious about other nationalities, and wherever you're from, you'll meet an enthusiastic audience.

Asian or African nationals may meet an initial cold shoulder. This is pure naiveté on the part of those who choose to remain closed and unaware. There's nothing particularly wrong about an Asian or African in the eyes of a Czech, but because he knows so little about them he has a built-in fear and misunderstanding of them. It just takes a bit of conversation to break down the walls.

Racism

A vestige of non-thinking hungover from Communism is the inherent suspicion amongst many Czechs toward anything or anybody different. There is an undertone of latent racism and sexism in many Czechs, more due to naiveté than any real malice. There hasn't yet been much cultural exchange here other than the historical shoulder-rubbing with Germany, Austria, Slovakia, and more recently, Russia, all of whom are incidentally white peoples.

The Communists did organise student and worker exchanges – African nationals, especially those of Communist-sympathetic countries such as Angola, came to study at Czech universities and technical schools, and some Vietnamese came to work in commercial fields. Many of these choose to stay of their own accord, as conditions and opportunities are often better here than at home. The numbers are small, so whereas there are large numbers of African or Asian nationals in countries such the US, Britain, or France, Czechs are much less accustomed to seeing dark faces around town. It is extremely rare to have an openly racist incident. Sentiments, while frank, remain beneath the surface, and general attitudes are non-confrontational.

Much of the misunderstanding, or non-understanding, is due to the long held distaste for Gypsies in Eastern Europe. Romanies (their proper name) have lived a nomadic existence, both physical and cultural, in the Czech lands for centuries, have not assimilated into society, and thus remain outcasts. Society in general here has acknowledged them as permanent outsiders, and has attached a negative stigma which has been applied to all similarly dark-skinned peoples. The natural reaction of many Czechs to anyone not white is avoidance. There is something different about a dark-skinned person, which the average Czech would simply rather not know anything about. Think of it as simply an additional (and unfortunate) barrier to breaking the ice.

Once personal contact is established, you will encounter respect, but you will start to get a funny feeling that you're just not Czech and therefore you have unfortunately missed something somewhere.

SOCIAL ORGANISATION
City Life Versus Country Life
The perspective taken in most of this book is one centred on life in Prague, which is where most expatriates in the country are located. Prague is of course a big city, not comparable to New York or London in size, but in the Czech Republic, no other town even comes close. Many of the progressive attitudes and the positive economic changes

spoken of here are indicative of the advances being made throughout the country, though with a particular emphasis on the capital city. In a city that attracts so much attention from international businesses and tourists, it is a natural development, while in smaller towns and in the countryside, the changes are coming more slowly. Traditional ways are more adhered to, people are often more reluctant to accept change, and sometimes you may get the feeling that these are two different worlds. This means, of course, that where Prague is becoming increasingly more cosmopolitan and predictable, small towns retain their typical charm and hospitality.

FAMILY AND THE LIFE CYCLE

The family is the basic element in the social fabric, and society as a whole is structured around this unit.

Childhood

The state provides a generous maternity leave: new mothers are allowed several months of partly or fully paid leave before and after giving birth, and they are fully entitled to get their jobs back when they are capable of returning. Many women prefer, however, to raise children them-selves, without relying on child support. This again is adherence to traditional ways, and in fact many Czech women look down on the Western tendency to continue career advancement while there are young children to raise. It's not just a matter of mouths to feed, it's a matter of raising children in a close knit and well balanced family.

Where the mother may take several months or years off work to raise a family, and the father is generally expected to provide the income to do so, the development of the family is a wholesome and integrative affair. Both parents assist in all aspects of raising the children, from teaching values, to helping with homework, to taking ski vacations in winter. Czechs are very conscious of being independent and well rounded, and to achieve this, a healthy family dynamic is considered essential. While divorce certainly does occur, many Czechs are shocked and dismayed at the high rates of it in the West. Families very rarely have more than two children, perhaps due to space limitations – nearly all families live in small flats, and it's not unusual for children of the opposite sex to share a bedroom throughout their time living at home.

As parents take a serious and caring approach to the practice of raising children, so children are properly appreciative of them, and hence, obedient. Kids are not spoiled in any way, due in part to the fact that most families don't have the financial resources to buy expensive toys. Instead, the whole family participates in enjoying life together: going to the theatre, visiting the grandparents, and enjoying the outdoors.

Part of the task of raising children, of course, is administering punishment, and Czech parents can discipline with vigour. I've seen the following event unfold several times: a mother is dragging her toddler along the pavement, and the child falls because he can't keep up; His mother then yanks him back up, slaps him (not too hard), the child starts crying, she gets huffy, and off they go again. Destructive behaviour, no? Corporal punishment of this kind is not a social problem, though it does occur.

Staying in the same vein of crassness, it is a common amusing/revolting sight to walk past a mother on a busy street or in a park helping her toddler pee into a gutter. Prague's Wenceslas Square – a prime business/shopping/nightlife area – is one of the more popular locales. It's things like this that make you wonder, where is the sense of refinement?

Growing into Adulthood

As Czech society has been spared many of the pressures running rampant in the West, children have less to rebel against and less to feel obliged to conform to. Even adolescent rebellion is held in check: teens continue to respect their parents and enjoy being with them. Parents are therefore quite good about giving their children freedom as they mature.

Children receive state supported education until age 18 or so. The high school years are surprisingly specialised: at about age 14 children decide if they want to attend a *gymnázium* (secondary school) or a technical school. Universities are difficult to get into, and most are now introducing tuition costs which Czechs find hard to bear. As evidence of the Czech practical nature, a large percentage of university students opt for technical and business degrees.

It is not unusual for children to continue to live with their parents well after age 18. This is due in part to the chronic lack of housing in Prague and throughout the country. Those who do move out visit their parents regularly on the weekends well into their twenties and thirties, to get their weekly dose of home cooking and parental attention.

Marriage

As tradition dictates in many countries, Czechs often marry at a young age: women are often *vdaná* (literally, 'given') around the ages 20–23, while men are often *ženátý* (the word derives from *žena* – woman) by the age of 26 or so. This is changing rapidly, however, especially in Prague. It is perhaps over-generalising, and even insulting, to say that couples often get married soon after the woman becomes pregnant, as if this is the motivation they need to tie the knot, but I personally know of several such cases.

Life Expectancy

The average life expectancy is low in comparison with many Western nations. This could arguably be attributed to a less than perfectly healthy lifestyle: Czech cities suffer from terrible pollution, and the traditional Czech diet is rich in fatty meats and starch. Czechs also seem to consider death as a natural part of life, or simply an end to life, and they don't necessarily nurse the elderly with pharmaceuticals to sustain a bedridden existence. The elderly are held in high esteem, such that when they become incapable of taking care of themselves, they often move in with their children rather than heading off to a nursing home. Again, the family is the core of life, and one is expected to care for one's elderly parents just as one was cared for as a child. A person who has lived beyond the age of 70 is considered to have lived a full life, and because of this there are few regrets or grievances for those who pass away at a 'reasonable' age.

Sex

Anyone who has read Kundera, Škvorecký, or Hrabal may easily jump to the conclusion that Czechs are highly sensitised to their libidinal instincts. All three contemporary writers speak quite openly and shamelessly of sexual trysts, extramarital affairs, and the human instincts behind these. Perhaps because all three wrote within the context of political oppression, sex is used as a theme for personal freedom and individual expression. And though they rarely flaunt it, Czechs do seem to take a relatively loose approach to sexual relations. There always seem to be sly rumours of unfaithful husbands and wives, and foreign men often delight in the beauty and approachability of Czech women.

Don't let this affect your common sense, however. Czechs are easy going and liberal-minded, though the general rules governing romantic and sexual etiquette are the same here as in many other countries.

Homosexuality is still a hush subject, as most Czechs feel uncomfortable discussing it. It's not a religious matter here as it is in some countries, it's more something that is just 'not normal' and therefore disquieting to most. Gays and lesbians remain very much in the closet, and while there is no overt discrimination or animosity toward homosexuals, most Czechs would just prefer not to address the issue, and ultimately would simply prefer it not to even be an issue at all. Prague does have a fair number of gay clubs and bars, and the media (especially such Western publications as *The Prague Post)* is opening the floor to awareness and acceptance, but overall, there is no movement or social phenomenon to speak of.

The attitude toward homosexuals in the Czech Republic is similar to their feelings toward any social trend or phenomenon: it's just not really worth talking about. Czechs admire individuality and tend toward privacy, and they don't bother with talking just for the sake of talking; whether someone chooses to wear Levi's, or if someone has a partner of the same sex, it's their own business.

Women

It's the same with the feminist movement. Because men and women already occupy fairly equal positions in society, and because many women are happy enough with their traditional roles, there isn't a strong desire to address any feminist issues. One tenuous advantage to Communism, in fact, was that women were considered equal to men, at least on paper. What this meant was that women were expected and in some cases assigned to work in factories alongside male colleagues, though they also worked as doctors, professors, and accountants just as their male counterparts did. Women therefore don't overtly object to discrimination, because it doesn't really exist as a problem in this domain.

This, again, is the situation on paper. In reality, women in the Czech Republic suffer the same subtle prejudices as in any male dominated society. While employment is not discriminated upon the basis of sex, men still occupy most of the top positions. Even as the political correctness of the West is trying to soften the traditional male-female roles, men here are still expected to bring home the bacon, and women are still expected to cook it. If you are sensitive to such a world view, you may be quick to take offence at the still traditional roles that men and women play in the Czech Republic. You will likely object to some of the random comments you are bound to hear, though in fact no harm or seriousness is generally meant by it. In a way, they're just reinforcing their traditional roles with which they feel most comfortable.

You'll find, if invited to a Czech home for example, that the women do all the meal preparation while the men sit and talk. If you make an attempt to help out with chopping the onions, the man may say no, leave it, it's her business. At the same time, though, it is not a gruff action: the woman will see it as her responsibility, and the man will be very gracious, complimenting his wife on how well she cooks.

Men in this way are seen as respecting women and their sexuality. They don't look upon women as objects of lust, nor do they simply put them down as incompetent because they are women.

Chapter Three

DOING BUSINESS

Czechs are quickly re-learning the efficiency and prowess which brought them into the top eight world economies before World War II, and they are leading the way in post-Communist former Eastern Europe's rush into the market economy. To most, the dark days of censorship and oppression are merely a bad memory.

However, Communism did have a strong effect on mentality and the way of going about doing (or not doing) business, from which Czechs are slowly but surely extricating themselves. Though occasional absurdities remain, blame this not on Czech thinking but on Communist non-thinking. Quality, efficiency, and customer service were not practised in business from 1948 to 1989, so Czechs have only had a few years to learn these business techniques. The sudden lust for money is often tangled up in unfamiliarity with the process of earning it. Therefore be aware that the procedure for doing business is not always as clear as what you may be used to: a seemingly straightforward deal may come across unforeseen and inexplicable problems, while a supposed agreement may not be so sure after all.

You may find the pace of work to be agonisingly slow. In the former system where efficiency of production was irrelevant, getting the job done was a matter of getting around to it. Some workers, especially those who do not deal with Western firms, can be painfully slow at accomplishing a task. Offices commonly start to close early Friday afternoon as everyone heads out of town. And when somebody gets sick, even with a common cold or flu, he or she usually takes the entire week off, or even more. Of course this is sensible, allowing the body to recover and not to spread the germs, but it's almost laughable how health clinics are jammed at 8:00 am with people trying to get sick-leave notes signed by the doctor.

On the other hand, Czechs these days are working harder than ever, even to the detriment of family life. Standards are rising rapidly, and many predict the Czech Republic will eclipse the economies of some European Union countries in the not too distant future. The following observations and tips may be a bit on the critical side, and they may not apply to your new colleagues, especially those who are by now used to the game.

A FEW STARTERS

When it comes to doing business in the Czech Republic, the rules are essentially the same as in the West, though there are a few important subtleties that you must be aware of. You must have a good sense of how things are done here and in what ways they are different, and this takes a little time to absorb. One company manager I spoke with complains that his single greatest frustration is interpreting between his US corporate policies and the local conditions. This is certainly not a criticism of the Czechs: many Westerners come in thinking that their way is simply how it should be done, and they make the mistake of choosing not to perceive the reality here. Know your environment before you make judgments or decisions on it.

Time is not quite the critical factor in Czech business as it often is in other countries. Where some are constantly driven by deadlines and incentives, Czechs are a bit more laid-back about getting things accomplished, and this allows them the chance to send out feelers and explore other possibilities. Or perhaps conversely, it is their tendency to check out all the options and let ideas gel in their mind, which takes so much time and can lead to frustrations for those unfamiliar with the practice. You also have to remember that this is a foreign country, with a different language and different laws, and if you don't speak Czech and aren't thoroughly familiar with the local ways, it simply takes longer to get through it all.

Flexibility will be your greatest asset – accept the fact that things are not quite the same as what you are used to. One simple rule that I developed early on was to eliminate the concept of 'should' from my mind, and simply to accept things as they came. This is not to say expect the unexpected, or expect the worst; you'll usually achieve what you set out to do, though occasionally in an unanticipated manner.

Czechs realise that the system they have emerged from was an illogical, inhuman one, which suppressed personality and destroyed entrepreneurial spirit. They know that they need to adapt to Western business practice if they want to reintegrate with the international market economy and in many cases they already have. The younger generation especially is extremely flexible, willing, and able. At the same time, however, Czechs do know what they are doing and they are wary of outsiders coming in and monitoring, telling them how it should be done.

Establishing a Business Relationship

The most important thing to keep in mind is not to enter with a superiority complex. Many Westerners come in assuming that Czechs are still in the dark ages and need to be taught what to do and how to do it. This is an enormous mistake to make, first of all because it's not true, and secondly because Czechs don't take kindly to unsought council. Those who succeed socially and in business are those who respect their Czech colleagues and friends. Those who fail are those who make little or no attempt to mingle and appreciate the culture, who stick to their own communities, and who act haughtily in business deals. Any pretence of superiority will only meet silent refusal.

Because Czechs often base their business relationships on personal sentiment (see below), it is crucial that you establish cordial relations with your potential colleagues, partners, and clients. So the question here is, how to get on the other person's side?

It is very important to act genuinely, to present yourself as a real person. Czechs have an intuition and a deep appreciation for sensibility and sensitivity, and any pretence of condescension or inapproachability will immediately work against you.

Most meetings start off with a short, light prelude – a comment on the weather, or a slight self criticism (for example, "I got off at the wrong metro stop") will set you on the right track. An excellent introductory remark is a simple *dobrý den, těší mě* ("Hello, pleased to meet you") said in Czech. Even with a funny accent, it comes off well, and is endearing to the listener. But don't prolong it. Americans have a tendency to chitchat, acting as if you are close friends from the get-go. This can be conducive to friendly relations if presented in a genuine fashion, but don't linger on it – get down to business, and stick to formal language.

Be Aware of Emotions

Czechs are very conscious of feelings, in fact, many business transactions succeed or fail based on the opinions formed about one another. I work in the real estate business in Prague, and we often hear from landlords at the initial meeting: "I want a tenant who is *solidní*" – meaning they want someone who is not only financially stable, but also a reasonable person. When it comes to negotiating a contract, we often hear comments from the landlord such as, "Well, she seems like a nice person, I think we'll work something out" or conversely, "No, she's too difficult, I don't want any problems."

This is not necessarily to say that Czechs are emotional in business dealings. The average Czech is not outwardly emotional. Rather, he is inwardly conscious of feelings. This can be difficult to recognise. Non-response from the other party may well be an avoidance of the issue. Remember, Czechs tend to be non-confrontational, and snags or stumbling blocks in the course of a negotiation may become insurmountable walls. It is important to recognise the danger signs: lowered eyes and silence are a signal that there is a problem, which the other party may feel paralysed to overcome. If this happens, take a step back, make a light-hearted remark, and proceed from there. (More in Negotiating, below.)

MONEY

One effect of dulled sensitivity to business dealings is that Czechs often think only about their side of the deal. When it comes to money, I've heard it stated simply: *Češi chtějí dostat, ale ne vydělávat* – Czechs want to make money, but not earn it. In this sense, they can be extraordinarily efficient: they want your money, and they can be inordinately tough when trying to get it. They want it all, and they want it now.

There is a sense among some of having been cheated for the past 40 years. Now countries such as neighbouring Germany "have everything" and Czechs "have nothing." But some still seem to think that it should just be handed to them. One of the initial reactions to freedom in 1990 was disillusion: the material things they had wanted for so long were suddenly available, but well out of proportion to the average salary.

THE INDIRECT APPROACH

One thing you will gradually start to perceive is that some Czechs take an indirect approach in business dealings. Your calls may go unanswered, you may find there are hidden other people responsible for various aspects of the transaction, and you may soon get the feeling of being jerked around. There are a few reasons for this.

Some Czechs are still a little green when it comes to wheeling and dealing, and they are a bit nervous about taking steps which may be risky. They often take their fine old time, making sure they've thought it all out, and likely conferred with colleagues and friends to validate their concerns, before proceeding.

A comically typical negotiation procedure for a house or apartment, for example, goes something like this: Day 1, view property and discuss initial terms; Day 2, haggle on kitchen appliances and light fixtures, and discuss a revised rent price for providing these items; Day 3, haggle again on the price; Day 4, whoops! the landlord suddenly is 'ill' or 'out of town' (read: he's taking time to think about it), call again tomorrow; Day 5, at the contract signing, the landlord comes up with a new demand, that the rent should be adjusted according to inflation after the second year of the lease. Further haggling ensues, and in the end neither side is quite sure if they can trust the other.

Under Communism, responsibility was shattered along with the destruction of the individual. Where the goal was a society of equal people, the individual was a lost entity. Therefore, as Havel writes, the displacement of the self meant the loss of responsibility, and the practical manifestations of this were played out in the lifeless roles assigned to all members of society. In business, this meant the lower level workers simply did what they were told, middle management relayed the dictates of their superiors, and the top brass simply followed the Party line.

So now, taking responsibility for individual actions, and accepting the blame when something goes wrong, is a bit difficult to stomach; it's always somebody else's fault, and if you're not careful, it can quickly be turned back onto you. Instead of admitting failure or defeat, they often try to patch up the problem, covering it up so that it looks alright – remember, most Czechs want to avoid confrontation at all costs.

Many organisations, particularly government offices and formerly government owned businesses, still function under an intimidating bureaucracy. If you want efficiency you'd be advised to avoid these.

GETTING THE JOB DONE

Performing a task quite often involves finding your own way to get it done. Sometimes this is equally, if not more effective, and sometimes it turns into a comedy of errors.

The indirectness spoken of above is quite simply due to lack of experience; as one Czech colleague of mine says, we in the West have this concept of a market economy built in – we've always lived in a consumer oriented economy, and are naturally cognisant of the marketplace. Czechs are fast learners, however, and conditions are infinitely better now than they were in the early 1990s. You may be pleasantly surprised at the dedication of motivated employees. Keep in mind that Czechs are an inherently logical people; in some cases they only need to be taught how to follow the thought process through. Employees often respond to a task with a simple "OK," and they proceed to do what they are told, no more, no less. Effective management tactics to bring out the best involve opening the floor to discussion and debate. Brainstorming sessions, where all employees involved are on even keel, are enormously productive; workers are full of ideas, though they may hesitate to challenge an authority. It also helps to explain not only the what but the why when giving instructions – following the thought process through can awaken the logic within.

BEATING THE SYSTEM

Because Czechs never took Communism seriously, they developed ways around the system, and in this manner they are ready and able to overcome a real problem. They are very creative in a utilitarian perspective and they are good at getting what they want. Now that Western firms are so active in the Czech Republic, locals are leaping at the opportunities for career advancement and higher salaries. Some even have the sense that Westerners are here to exploit: amongst their many virtues, Czechs are crafty at getting your self-esteem and money.

NEGOTIATING

Most sources agree that negotiations are not always carried out fairly—they can be tough, as there is not always an inbuilt desire to please both sides. Again, it's a matter of thinking it all through – the demands that are placed comprise a long list of what your opposing number wants. The key difference is that when a Czech business-person presents an offer, it is not a basis for bargaining: the offer made is essentially what he expects to get. This is not to say there is no room for flexibility, but don't expect him to give in much.

Where one is generally accustomed to making an offer, having analysed the situation as thoroughly as possible, and leaving room for negotiation within that offer, a Czech may simply lay all his cards on the table, take it or leave it. Beyond that, he is probably waiting to see what more he can get from you. Counter-offers are rarely given: it's not a process of offer-and-counter-offer so much as offer-and-acqui-escence – and the cynics out there say he's always trying to pull you more and more towards his end of the deal.

The indirect approach mentioned above comes into play during negotiating sessions. Czechs are exceedingly polite in most business situations, and this can even get in the way of productive haggling. If a sticking point comes up you may notice your counterpart avoiding your eyes, speaking to a third party instead of directly to you, and taking a sort of roundabout approach to the deal. The topic of conversation may change, or a weighty silence may ensue, while he lets the latest thought turn over in his mind. You may find yourself having to lead the whole negotiation, easing the discussion along while trying to cover all relevant points.

One company manager I spoke with outlines it thus: the Western business-person often infuses a sense of urgency into a deal, while the Czech counterpart often doesn't have the same constraints, so he sits and waits. The Westerner then gets nervous and starts to cave in more and more until the final outcome is decidedly in the other guy's favour. This is a big mistake, especially when the Westerner does have some leverage. Remember, your Czech partner wants the deal as much as you do. If you approach him on an even keel and proceed with reason, you will get a better result.

Remember to keep your cool, to listen calmly and patiently. It's fine to express disapproval, but do so gently; always retain a measure of respect for your interlocutor. Don't ever give an appearance of unfriendliness or condescension – Czechs pick up on this immediately, and respond in one of two ways: either save face at all costs or, conversely, back away and drop everything. In either case, you're up against a wall. If the negotiations start to get tense, you may find the other party becoming defensive, bristling at the notion of having to relent in any way. If he turns non-communicative, he is probably contemplating and may take a while to come back with a reasonable response.

Don't acquiesce too much unless it is really necessary, or he may find you too soft. Retain your position of leverage. A bit of bullying, done gently, can take you far. The best position to be in is when you're very close to finishing the deal, having accepted many of his terms (assuming they are acceptable) from the outset. From here, he'll hold onto his demands even though he sees the end in sight. If you've established a good business accord, you'll find it much easier to wind things up productively.

As a last resort, a threat to just walk away from it all will often scare him and he'll simply give in. He is being as tough as he can, but if he perceives it falling through, he may well drop his hold-out requests. I once was brokering a deal for a client who, in the midst of a final sticking point, looked at his watch and realised he had to make a phone call. He jumped up to find the number in his jacket, which his adversary perceived as him walking out of the deal, and he immediately dropped his demand.

Please note that these again are generalisations. Many Czech businesspeople are perfectly comfortable with straightforward negotiations, and you often won't notice any difference in procedure.

FORMAL AND LEGAL MATTERS

The final contract is the most important element to any transaction and you should never feel at ease until you have this signed. Once the contract is signed, it is honoured to the best of one's abilities. Czechs are respectful of this formality. You can rest easy when the contract is signed, but there is still the issue of getting the money. Cash in hand is the only guarantee, even an invoice does not insure payment, as you may well have to follow up on it to get your reward.

The Czech legal system is as confounding as anywhere, though it is a reliable institution. The Czech Republic in fact was well ahead of its east European neighbours in drawing up new legislation for trade and taxation, and it continues to introduce progressive measures in a determined attempt to leave the discrepancies of the former system behind. Having a good lawyer who is familiar with both Czech law and Western practices is essential.

One thing that Western companies often overlook in expanding to the Czech Republic is that there are different laws and indeed a different language governing the whole operation. Contracts written in English or other languages are valid, though if there is a Czech version as well, it prevails in case of dispute. All contracts must be carefully checked to insure that they correspond with Czech legal provisions.

Bribes and Other Payoffs

Contrary to what many people seem to believe, 'hush money' is not the order of business here. Bribes and under-the-table payments do occur, but they are regarded as exceedingly low-class, reminiscent of Communist days. One of the major news stories of 1995 was a seven million Kč (US$275,000) 'bribe' accepted by the Czech minister of privatisation; the population reacted with disgust. This is considered an extreme, a deviation in which Communists, mafiosi, and corrupt businessmen engage. Czechs feel they ought to be above this, and in most cases they are. Don't even consider straying off the ethical course in regular business transactions.

Under-the-table payments and little favours are similarly regarded as unethical, though in many cases, it is the easiest way to get things done. The comedy of it all is that one really ought not to participate in such deals, though many do. In another example from real estate, I was once part of a deal in which the official rent price was written in the contract as half the real amount, while the remainder was declared as 'payment for services.' This allowed the landlords to escape the higher tax bracket in which the full rental amount would have put them.

Telephones are a chronic problem in the country, and many people resort to paying off someone they know to get more lines installed. It's not purely a technical shortfall: phone lines can be installed, but the waiting list is so long it will still take years to fulfil the demand. So what do you do if you need more phone lines? Get in touch with a friend who knows somebody in the phone company. For a 'bribe' of a few hundred dollars, special installation can be arranged.

The police themselves often work under a quiet system of bribery, and for those willing to veer off the straight-and-narrow, paying off the traffic police can save you hundreds of crowns. On more than one occasion I've been pulled over for a moving violation, which should have met a fine equal to about US$40. Just a little bit of protest and plea for sympathy though, and the cop let me off with an $8 'gimme,' which I assume went straight into his pocket.

You'll notice that many financial transactions are carried out in cash, and there are two reasons for this. First, there is no adequate system of credit established in the Czech Republic, so personal cheques are extremely limited. Second, and more importantly, payments in cash can slip through the accounting books.

BUSINESS FUNCTIONS

The 'business lunch' is a common social interlude, though it is not commonly used as a medium for meeting and negotiating. More often, colleagues head down to a local pub for a quick bite around noontime. The experience is not necessarily one of exciting food and enlightening conversation, though. You will likely soon tire of the

A Czech business lunch is usually an informal affair and may take place at the local pub.

67

same old meat-and-potatoes, and the locals often down their meals as quickly as possible, seeming to focus merely on the plate and on getting it all in.

There aren't too many activities in the way of company get-togethers, parties, and the like. Office parties may spark up on the occasion of somebody's birthday or name-day, and colleagues often head to the pub for a beer or two after hours, where they continue to discuss business or develop a social rapport in a more casual manner. In general, though, Czechs keep their public and private lives separate.

Exhibitions and trade fairs are very important in business. Prague and Brno both have large convention and exhibition centres, which are fully booked months and even years in advance. Business-people take advantage of the opportunity to make new contacts on a face-to-face basis, and if you want to do the same, you'd be well advised to follow suit.

BUSINESS FORMALITIES

Czechs have a strong concept of polite behaviour, and in most situations (shop assistants and waiters sometimes excepted) you will find them humbly, almost painfully polite. Aligning yourself with this simple fact is a key to making a good impression. Refer to the sections on polite expressions and body language in the chapter on Communicating, and remember the importance of a firm handshake.

Business cards *(vizitky)* are an important instrument. All Czechs have them, and they tend to distribute them generously. Whenever you are presented with a card, be sure you have one of your own to offer; it's a small token, but it makes you look much more professional in their eyes.

Office Hours

Czechs tend to start and finish their day about an hour or two earlier than most. Offices thus open as early as 7:00 or 8:00 am and close by 4:00 or 5:00 pm, though the influx of Western business, and the general Czech drive to success, has affected these hours. Shops open anywhere from 8:00 to 10:00 am, and generally close by 6:00 pm. Bakeries, grocery stores and news-stands open at 6:00 or 7:00 am. More and more shops are staying open later and opening on weekends. Peak hours on the public transport systems are 5:00 to 8:00 am and 2:00 to 5:00 pm.

Public Holidays

- January 1   New Year's Day
-                 Easter Monday
- May 1   Labor Day
- May 8   Liberation Day
- July 5   St. Cyril and Methodius Day
- July 6   Jan Hus Day
- October 28   Independence Day
- December 25   Christmas Day
- December 26   St. Stephen's Day

Chapter Four

COMMUNICATING

LANGUAGE

One of the most difficult aspects to living in a foreign country, of course, is the language. In the Czech Republic especially, you'll find it extremely frustrating to live day by day if you don't acquire at least a basic vocabulary. Relying on friends and colleagues to interpret for you is a poor means of getting by, and you'll soon find yourself floundering if you don't make an attempt.

Native English speakers are fortunate that this has rapidly become the 'international language,' and in the Czech Republic as most anywhere, many people are able to communicate in English. Most well-educated persons speak some English, and many do so with near-fluency. The universality of the English language is probably due to the expanse of the former British Empire, whose former colonies, including the United States, have become important international powers. British and American pop culture have undoubtedly influenced many; in fact many Czechs confess to having started learning English through the Beatles!

It is arrogant and wrong, however, to assume that everyone you meet will understand English, and that you will be able to get by with it. True, you'll make yourself understood somehow, but to spend time in a foreign country without trying to assimilate into something so basic as communicating is not only an injustice to yourself, but also a mark of disrespect to your host people.

That said, you are up against a monstrous task, for Czech is an extraordinarily complex language that takes incredible patience and stamina to learn. The *Book of Lists* in fact rates Czech as one of the most difficult languages on the planet. So, many foreigners living in Prague become so intimidated by it that they quickly give up. This is undoubtedly compounded by the fact that many are too busy with their regular jobs and family and social calendars to really apply themselves to the task, and also because so many of the Czechs they meet are eager to improve their command of English. As understandable as this is, keep in mind that your standing is raised a hundredfold if you are able to communicate with Czechs in their own tongue.

If you must communicate in English, heed the following basic rules of courtesy. Always ask first if the other person speaks English. Speak slowly and clearly, but not overly so: many who claim to speak only a little English in fact speak very well, and too much slow motion acting comes across as condescending. Those with North American accents should be aware that many Czechs learned textbook British English and therefore have a hard time deciphering the American twang.

Because Czech is so difficult, and because it is (unfortunately) so insignificant outside of the country itself, Czechs are extraordinarily receptive and appreciative of anyone who makes the remotest attempt to acquire even a basic vocabulary. The utterance of even a few random words is invariably met with, "Oh! you speak good Czech!" which is wonderful for the ego but can lure you into a false sense of security.

71

LEARNING CZECH

The formal language that Jan Hus systematised in the early 1400s has been noted by linguists as the perfect legal language, as the subtleties of expression leave no room for doubt as to their meaning. This of course means that it is especially difficult to master. Even Czech children need to be taught the nuts and bolts before they are able to use it properly.

It takes a lot of textbook-work to make headway; Czech is not a language that you can simply "pick up" without systematic study. Progress is invariably slow, and you'll likely only notice it long after you've been in the country and "suddenly" find yourself understanding bits and pieces. It's always easier to follow a conversation on a topic with which you're familiar; listening to the radio or picking up on a random conversation is always the hardest thing to do.

Many students choose to enrol in a language course to learn the fundamentals of grammar and pronunciation, and this is a good idea, at least in the beginning. Real learning, though, is achieved only through independent study and willpower.

The obvious starting points are pronunciation, basic greetings, food, and numbers. Learn how to say hello *(dobrý den)*, please *(prosím)*, thank you *(děkuji)*, and learn a few critical nouns and verbs, and you'll have a foot in the door. Then you can try to tackle the complexities of verb conjugation, declension of nouns and pronouns, formal and informal speech, and the subtleties of expression.

THE CZECH LANGUAGE

The Czech language is a member of the Slavic family of languages, and is therefore similar in many ways to Russian, Polish, and Slovak. (There is no relation to German other than a few words and names which have jumped the border). It uses the same alphabet as English (unlike Russian, which uses the Cyrillic alphabet) and is perfectly phonetic once you know the letter sounds.

Letters and Pronunciation

Where the English alphabet has 26 letters, Czech has 40. Marks above letters render them completely different letters: *c* and *č* are considered different letters, and there are lots of lines and hooks, to the point where there is scarcely a word without such extra signs. These are easy enough to pronounce once you know the rules, though there is one letter, ř, which is so difficult that even children have to be taught properly how to say it. It's a hard 'r,' rolled but once, followed immediately by 'zh,' and it's all one sound.

Strict phonics means that each letter has a specific sound, and therefore each word has a perfect pronunciation based upon the letters in it. Once you learn the letters, you can pronounce any word. This is not to say that Czech words are easy to pronounce, however! Whereas English words are formed with the whole mouth, Czech words are for the most part formed with the front of the mouth; the tongue and the lips can quite easily get entangled as you try to get everything out. Czechs consider their language very 'soft;' it contains many 'sh' and 'zh' sounds, for example, whose soothing sonority is admired. At the same time, though, there are some awful consonant clashes in words such as *skříň* ('skrzheenye') and *chci* ('khtsee'), which take a lot of practice to get right, and still end up spilling out of the front teeth in a confused splutter.

Czech words often contain a lot of consonants, and the letters 'k' and 'z,' uncommon in English, seem to turn up with frustrating regularity in Czech. Two letters, 'l' and 'r,' can function as syllables, producing some marvellous words such as *vlk, krk, mlč,* and *smrt.*

All Czech words are accented on the first syllable. This makes it easy to know how to pronounce a word, though long words seem to dwindle off at the end. The name Navrátilová, for example (as in Martina the tennis player – she's originally Czech) is always mispronounced internationally.

Formal and Informal Speech

When your command of the language progresses beyond the 'hello' and 'one beer please' stage, you'll start to notice differences between formal and informal speech. As in most other European languages (except English) there are different words for 'you' and different conjugations of the verb that follows. When speaking to friends, close acquaintances, family members, and young children, use the informal *ty.* When meeting people for the first few times, and when addressing business contacts and those older than yourself, always use the formal *vy.* (This *vy* is also used as 'you' plural, even when addressing a group of friends). Confusing the two can be very embarrassing for both sides. You would never address a client or the bank teller as *ty,* and you would seem extremely stiff to address a friend as *vy.* Not only must you be aware of which form of 'you' to employ, you must also choose which greetings to use: *dobrý den* and *nashledanou* are the formal 'hello' and 'goodbye,' while *ahoj* and *čau* are spoken to friends and family.

It can be difficult to ascertain when a relationship has developed to such a point that you can switch to the informal. Always address elders and superiors in the formal, even if they use the informal with you, unless they specifically say that you can be less proper. In office relationships and with friends, Czechs usually switch to the informal after the first meeting, to establish a friendly accord. Still, you shouldn't use the informal address until the other person initiates it – this can be a funny event in itself, when the Czech person may ask rhetorically, *mužeme se tykat?* (we can use the 'ty' form?). This momentous occasion is then celebrated with a handshake and possibly even a drink.

Conjugation of Verbs and Declension of Nouns and Pronouns

Verbs are conjugated according to a system of models; any given verb belongs to one of five models, and there are different endings for each based on the personal pronoun. Fortunately, there are only three tenses: simple past, simple present, and simple future.

Not only do verb endings change according to use, but nouns and pronouns also change according to context. For anyone who has not studied Latin, German, or Russian, this is probably the single most confounding aspect to the language. Even your own name changes according to its use in the sentence, and while it's easy to figure out who Billa Clintona is, it's a difficult task to get it right when you're doing the talking. After several years of constant use, I still manage to get the endings wrong half the time. The trick is to memorise, or recognise, patterns. The last letter of the word is your indication. Any word that ends in 'o,' for example, is declined according to its model, so you can start to make educated guesses without specifically memorising the model for every word.

The Beauty Of It

Despite, or perhaps because of, all the complexity, Czech is an extremely descriptive and beautiful language, and in this way is very practical as well. Many words have a logical basis; for example the word for entrance, *vchod*, literally means 'walk in,' and the word for exit, *východ*, means 'walk out;' a farmer is a *zemědělec* – 'earth maker.'

The months are all derived from their relative elements: January, *leden*, means 'ice;' May, *květen*, means 'flower' or 'blossom,' and November, *listopad*, means literally 'leaves fall.' The days of the week are similarly descriptive: Wednesday is *středa* – 'middle,' while Sunday is the perfectly apt: *neděle* – 'do nothing.' The poeticism of the language is one of the reasons Czechs are so enamoured of it.

Czech names are often very descriptive as well, even to the point of silliness. Many Czech names are not just names, they are words with meanings. Some of the more common family names, in fact, are Small *(Malý)* and Black *(Černý)*. Stranger, though, are names you occasionally come across, such as Lardspread *(Škvarek)*, Excellent *(Výborný)*, Scrotum *(Šourek)*, Didn't-eat-dinner *(Nevečeřal)* and Jump-to-the-fields *(Skočdopole)*. These are real names! Women's surnames are always changed to the feminine or possessive ending forms of the male name. So all women you meet will have names ending in *-ová* or *-á*.

Czech uses a lot of diminutives; in fact, virtually every Czech word can have an ending tacked on to it to make it sound small and quaint. Where English has a few such words, like booklet or birdy, any Czech word can be diminutised, some for no apparent reason. Why bother calling a fax machine a 'little fax machine' when it's not? In some ways such diminutives serve a practical function, though: a spoon, *lžíce*, becomes *lžička* when it's a teaspoon.

Polite Expressions

Whenever you need to approach someone to ask for help or information, don't launch into the discussion without the standard *dobrý den* greeting. This should then be followed with a respectful *prosím Vás*, which is a step above *prosím*, translating roughly as 'I ask of you' or 'if you please' – it serves to acknowledge that you are asking a favour of the other person. Remember that Czechs have a built-in sense of politesse. Even if the people you address may look dour and nasty (especially those in low-paying government or sales clerk jobs) a *prosím Vás* will help to swing them over to your side.

People of many cultures often follow up the 'hello' with a 'how are you?' though Czechs rarely use this artificial space-filler unless they really mean it. Where English-speakers almost always throw out a 'how's it going?' or a 'how's everything?' and the French commonly ask 'ça va?' usually only expecting to hear the standard response, 'I'm fine thanks,' Czechs tend to hear the question literally. So if you ask a colleague on a Monday morning, 'How are you?' (*jak se máš* – informal; *jak se máte* – formal) he may respond with, 'Oh, I'm feeling a bit ill this morning' or 'Yes, thank you, I had a nice weekend.' If you ask a first-time acquaintance or business contact, he will probably express surprise that you're already asking a personal question. Reserve the question for friends for whom you are genuinely interested in the answer.

Czechs do note the superficiality of small talk that many foreign cultures are wont to engage in, and they identify this with lack of real personality. In business settings, try not to broach personal matters beyond the topic at hand. The ho-ho guffaws that Americans in particular are so good at don't go over well here at all.

Titles

The use of titles is strictly adhered to. On business cards and on door signs you usually see the person's name accompanied by his or her professional degree – there is a great respect for education here. Therefore, it is important in both spoken and written communication to address the person with his or her appropriate title. In fact, professionals are often referred to as Mr. Doctor *(pan doktor)* or Mrs. Professor *(paní profesorka)*, as a measure of respect, a small form of flattery. One of the most common accompaniments to a name is the classification 'ing.' which stands for *ingenýr*, the equivalent of a business or technical degree, which many Czechs possess.

First names are never used in business situations, except with colleagues and long-established contacts. Westerners often switch to the first name basis after the initial contact, to establish what they hope to be a friendly, healthy relationship. In Czech business this only happens once you're very well acquainted. Always use the last name and precede it with a *pan* or *paní* (Mr. or Mrs./Ms.).

Common Courtesies

Don't commence your babbling away in English unless you are sure the other person speaks English. If you don't know, ask politely, *Mluvíte anglický?* ('Do you speak English?').

Even if you don't speak Czech, you should at least learn how to say thank you and goodbye. Unfortunately, 'thank you' is one of the most difficult words to pronounce correctly in Czech. A simple thank you is *děkuji* ('dyekuee'); if you want to emphasise this, for example if the person went out of his way to help you, you can say *děkuji Vám*, literally, 'I thank you,' or *děkuji moc krát*, literally 'thank you many times.' Czechs don't get too worked up by formalities, though being able to communicate these simple pleasantries always works in your favour. When taking leave of someone, always remember to say goodbye – *nashledanou*.

These general tips are especially important in telephone conversations, when personal contact is more limited – so be on your best behaviour!

SLANG AND SWEARING

Czechs don't seem to curse as often or as loudly as others. The four-letter words that we tend to utter so frequently in English sound especially hard and vulgar in Czech. Czechs are struck by the excessive rudeness of swearing, and usually temper their vocabulary or murmur it under their breath. Needless to say, swearing is reserved for light-hearted communication between close friends and acquaintances. If you really get upset and start swearing at someone in public, you'll attract a host of shocked onlooking eyes.

There is an amusing word in Czech, *vůl*, which is spoken frequently and must be dealt with delicately. A *vůl* is an ox, which seems harmless in itself, but the implications this word has are significant. To call someone an ox is to call them a lowdown, moronic boor, so of course it is extremely insulting; at the same time though, the word is used almost casually amongst close friends as a silly quip to acknowledge camaraderie, almost as Americans use the expression 'man.' It's almost a challenge to say *ty vole* ('you ox') to someone, and it is only used with someone you're very comfortable with, yet within these circles it's spoken with almost careless abandon. Women please note that the expression is extremely masculine. To call someone a cow *(kráva)* is similarly insulting, though is often apt for some service staff!

Those with religious inclinations will be surprised and even shocked to hear the Lord's name taken in vain with reckless alacrity. Remember Czechs are not a religious people overall, so using Christ as a scapegoat is a common form of relieving tension or expressing anger. Once your ears are attuned to Czech speech, you'll start to hear the profane *Ježíše Marie!* ('Jesus Mary') or *Pane Bože!* ('Mr. God'), spoken to mean anything from 'Oh no' to 'C'mon, what now!' to 'What the hell is going on!' Don't take offence.

You may be shocked to hear the expression *fakt jo!* which sounds dangerously like the most offensive sendoff imaginable in English. *Fakt* means 'fact,' and *jo* is equivalent to 'yeah,' so the meaning is something like 'really!' or 'I can't believe it!' Unfortunately Czechs do have the F-word in their vocabulary, so be careful who you may choose to use it on; likewise, don't take offence if someone says it to you.

Mind-Boggling Tongue Twisters

Due to its heavy reliance on crashing consonances, Czech has some of the most difficult tongue-twisters of any language. Even getting through these slowly once is a chore.

The most commonly known, and perhaps most bizarre due to its entire lack of vowels, is the relatively simple *strč prst skrz krk* – 'stick a finger through your neck.' Moving on in silliness of meaning is this warm-up phrase: *Kmotře Petře, nepřepepřte toho vepře* – 'Godfather Peter, don't over-pepper this pig.' All hell breaks loose, however, and the spittle goes flying while attacking the following: *třistatřicettři stříbrných stříkaček stříkalo přes třistatřicettři stříbrných střech,* whose meaning is secondary to its simple existence, 'three hundred thirty three silver hoses shoot over three hundred thirty three silver roofs.' A children's favourite is *od poklopu ku poklopu Kyklop koulí koulí* – 'from manhole cover to manhole cover Cyclops runs around;' meanwhile adults manoeuvre through *nenaolejuje-li tě Julie, naolejuji- tě já* – 'if Julia doesn't oil you, I'll oil you.'

LANGUAGE SCHOOLS

For those who want to learn the Czech language, there are several language schools in Prague offering Czech lessons. Three to try are:
*   SPUSA (Society of Friends of the USA), Navrátilqva 2, Prague 1, tel. 24 91 28 49/50
*   Angličtina Express, Záhřebská 32, Prague 2, tel. 25 68 33
*   Berlitz, V Jámě 8, Prague 1, tel. 2421 3185 or Na Poříčí 12, tel. 2487 2052

BODY LANGUAGE

For a people not given to emotional displays, body language is not a particularly noteworthy aspect in communicating. In fact, it's more helpful to be aware of what Czechs don't do that many other people do in order to avoid offence.

Greetings and their Related Civilities

When greeting someone, anyone, a firm handshake is an appropriate, respectful gesture. In business settings, the handshake is always accompanied with the greeting *dobrý den* (hello); in social meetings, a simple *ahoj* or *čau* (hi) usually suffices instead of the handshake. In a group of people, men always offer their hands to women first, and it is perfectly appropriate for men and women to shake hands, even in social settings.

More physical displays of affection are rare. Men almost never greet male friends with anything more than a handshake; an affectionate hug between men is still seen as a bit queer (see section on sexual relations). Women greeting female friends do occasionally accompany the greeting with a kiss on the cheek, though again, this is not everyday practice.

The kiss on the cheek between men and women, as practised in many European countries, is reserved for extra-friendly or romantic relations. When greeting a member of the opposite sex, do not make the move to kiss him or her on the cheek unless you are absolutely comfortable with the person and your standing with him or her. Similarly, men only kiss women on the hand in a semi-joking cultural affectation. Any lip-puckering has a romantic/sexual connotation and should be avoided unless respectfully intended.

While physical contact is limited, visual contact is very important. When shaking someone's hand, always look them square in the eye. It is said that the eye is the window on the soul, and to Czechs, this is an important means of contact.

When saying goodbye, the handshake is repeated, accompanied by several *nashledanou*s or *čau*s. If there are more than two people in the group, it is common for everyone to shake hands with everyone else, though true to their practical nature, Czechs don't make a circus of it. In business meetings, it is common to follow up the goodbye with a comment that you were glad to have met the person, to thank them, and to perhaps mention that you'll meet again next week.

Other Body Language

Always remember to maintain eye contact. As in many places, this establishes friendship and equality between friends and business associates alike. Remember especially to look the other person in the eye when toasting a drink; it is considered very bad form to simply

watch the glasses clink, as if the drink is more important than the person. (More about this in the section on pub culture).

International hand signals such as the thumbs-up, the 'OK' thumb-and-index-finger circle, and the raised middle finger, are recognised by all but not actively used.

One body motion you will notice quite often is the exasperated arms-thrown-up-at-the-shoulders. This is usually a direct 'What the hell are you doing?' or 'What the hell's going on?' seen regularly in traffic intersections in Prague. The exclamation is usually accompanied by a helpless, 'Well, what do you expect?' sort of shrug.

STANDARDS OF APPEARANCE

True to their humble nature, Czechs tend to groom, dress, walk, and talk as modestly as possible, obliging themselves of the necessities of good appearance but not going far beyond that. (President Havel himself is often seen in a Rolling Stones T-shirt.) Czechs are not obsessed with physical appearance, and the trends in dress that so many societies go through are for the most part insignificant here, although fashion trends are catching on, particularly amongst young women.

Business attire is similar to most anywhere. Sharp dress is not necessary, so long as it corresponds with the basic coat and tie or skirt and blouse theme. You see lots of greys and browns, but then you see some wild colour schemes as well: purple dress jackets and white socks are not uncommon. Don't try to impress with grand appearances in Armani suits and full-length furs: Czechs are not at all ostentatious in this way, and they don't look kindly on artificial displays. They are much more interested in what's inside.

Image

Czechs do, however, have a new concept of image. Many have exciting new roles now, and a few choose to play them out in almost comical fashion, picking up the swagger and the accents of the Western businessmen they observe. This often comes off in exaggerated fashion: some seem to take themselves too seriously, and the style is as abrasive here as similar behaviour anywhere.

Chapter Five

SOCIALISING

MEETING AND BEING MET

Czechs tend to stick with the groups of people they know and feel comfortable with. They are generally eager to let more people into their social circle (particularly if they are foreign), but it often takes a certain catalyst to open the doors of friendship. Relationships springing from within offices, schools, or friends of friends are the easiest to form, as one feels more comfortable as part of this larger organisation. Within such social organisations, Czechs are open, friendly, and accommodating, and, assuming you have such a network at hand, you'll find Czechs to be a cordial and amicable bunch. Meeting people at random, however, is much more intimidating, so use the resources you have.

You will have a distinct advantage in simply being foreign – it's surprising how interested they can be in you. But then, you'll likely get tired of the same old conversation starters, such as the standard "Where are you from?" and "How do you like Prague?"

CONVERSATION

The very fact of your being in the Czech Republic is probably going to be your greatest conversation piece as you get to know someone, especially if you are living outside of Prague. Conversation in any social setting will likely revolve around cultural issues. Talking about your own interests, your national customs and traditions, and your family will always meet an attentive audience.

Where Czechs are innately curious about foreign things, they also take great pride and become wonderfully open to you when they see you taking an interest in their culture. Thus, your best inroads into winning one's affections are to express an interest and excitement in them. This can also be an excellent opportunity to find out more about the country's history, art, and social customs. This means a lot of question asking in the beginning, but later, when you start to know a few things about Czech culture, your friends and the people you meet will be delighted at your knowledge of their little country.

Politics is generally avoided as a conversation topic, as most Czechs simply aren't interested in it. Perhaps it's the built-in distrust and sarcasm on the part of most Czechs that precludes political debate of any kind. Whatever the reason though, they pay little attention to local or international politics, so the conversation would soon die in its tracks. Steer clear of any discussion of the Communist era, despite the interest that you may have in it. Czechs are fighting as hard as they can to forget about it. They may bring it up themselves, though only in the context of today's changes.

A well advised suggestion can be made here when conversing with Czechs on any level: do not patronise. Many Westerners make the mistake of coming in and trying to impose values on Czechs and Czechs often complain that some foreigners come in with a 'you monkeys' attitude. Once again, this is a well educated and a self conscious nation, proud of its achievements and its identity, and any showing of disrespect or superiority on your part will backfire immediately.

EATING AT SOMEONE'S HOME

Being invited to dinner at a Czech person's home is a rare event, and should be jumped at because of it. Because an invitation to a Czech home is such a special occasion, you should carry yourself with appropriate humility and respect, as you will be treated with considerable honour. Try to determine before you go whether this is indeed a dinner invitation or just an evening get-together, especially if it's planned for late afternoon or late evening, or you may wind up eating pretzels all night. They do tend to invite friends over just for a chat every once in a while.

A token gift is always happily received, though it's not expected. Do not overdo it. Any offering of something expensive or exceptionally personal will meet with recoil: your host may then feel obliged to reciprocate with something of equal or higher value, and you may well find yourself presented with beautiful books and family heirlooms. It's only a token gesture anyway, so keep it simple. A bottle of wine or liquor is your safest bet. If you have any particular trinkets from your home country, they can be given to symbolise the cultural exchange.

Flowers hold a particularly romantic, even sexual connotation here, so a gift of a bouquet of flowers may be perceived as a bit untoward, unless, of course, that is the point. Just note that Czechs usually don't take flowers out of the plastic wrap; if you are ever offered flowers you should adhere to the same practice.

You will be treated royally. From the moment you enter the home you will be offered a drink, and from the moment you finish it you will be offered another. Small appetisers, such as chips or nuts, may be served, and during the meal you will be constantly doted upon. Don't offer to help with any aspect of preparation or cleaning up. You are the honoured guest, and your host is expected to properly care for you. Any overly-friendly gestures, such as offering to help clear the dishes, are perceived as a sort of sign of discontent, as if the hosts had overlooked it themselves, and can be quite embarrassing.

When settling down at the table, a simple *dobrou chut'* (enjoy your meal) suffices as a toast; the host will always say it with an honest hope that you will like the food. It is therefore imperative that you praise the meal at some point during eating. This is always a conversation starter anyway, as you may well want to comment on its preparation, while your hosts will invariably want to discuss your personal and national eating habits. It is generally good form to accept a second helping, which will likely be offered, even if you ask for just a little bit. Let yourself be spoiled; when you really can't take any more, say something like, "It's really excellent, but I just I can't handle any more."

After the meal, you'll probably move back to the living room for conversation and coffee, and perhaps a glass of Becherovka. You should always accept what is offered, or if you'd prefer not to have it, suggest a glass of water instead – they will always feel obliged to serve you something, so to say, "Oh, no, I don't want to trouble you" is beside the point. More conversation will follow, and you'll probably go through photo albums and listen to music.

INVITING CZECHS TO YOUR HOME

Pay special attention to returning the favour with an invitation of your own. It is indeed a friendly gesture, though note the socioeconomic differences between your culture and your hosts, if such a disparity does exist. Keep in mind that most Czechs still live in small, humble apartments and their salaries are likely lower than your own. If you live in a big house or apartment paid for on company money, you'll likely only instill a sense of embarrassment if you invite Czech friends over. Czechs are therefore more likely to invite you back again, to avoid what they may sense as a potentially uncomfortable situation.

Nevertheless, they are innately curious, and if you do feel comfortable enough to invite a Czech friend over, try to prepare a meal typical of your own country. If you are, say, Brazilian or Japanese, this is a marvellous opportunity to turn them on to something completely different; if you're American, this is a good chance to prove that American food is more than just pizza and hamburgers. They will undoubtedly want to see your books and hobbies, photos of your country, your family; again, cultural relations are at the forefront.

DINING ETIQUETTE

One must always precede the first bite of a meal with a proper incantation to the life giving qualities of food. Just as the French say *bon appetit*, Czechs make sure to say *dobrou chut'* as a form of blessing. The expression doesn't quite translate into English, though we don't have one of our own anyway, a fact that Czechs find almost barbaric. The literal meaning is 'good taste,' and it's sometimes preceded with *přeju Vám* ... ("I wish you ..."). Be sure to respect this formality, and when your host or dinner guest bestows it upon you, respond with the same, or use the French *bon appetit*; it's widely understood. Your non-fluent host may try to be clever and proclaim in English, "good taste!" to which a simple nod of the head is appropriate.

Czechs rarely offer a speech-like toast. The proper action is to raise the glass and pronounce *nazdráví!*, ("to health!") at the first drink. (A common linguistic confusion amongst foreigners lies in the similarity of the words *nazdráví* and *nádraží*, which means "train station;" you'll get an appreciative laugh by purposely mixing them up.)

Czechs often simply clink the glasses and say *ahoj* or *čau* ("hi" – this serves as an acknowledgment of friendship, and is said with a sparkle in the eye and a satisfied smile.

Czechs always eat with the knife in the right hand and fork in the left; it's practical. Those who attempt to cut and feed the mouth all in one fork motion are seen as exceedingly classless.

The napkin always remains neatly folded on the table, not on the lap. There is no apparent reason for this though, especially as many pub and restaurant napkins are merely a cheap piece of almost non-absorbent paper. When you've finished eating, it's considered good form to lay the knife and fork parallel on the plate and to scrunch up the napkin and drop it on the plate as well. In more formal settings, it's acceptable to place your napkin on your lap and leave it on the table when they clear the plate.

— Chapter Six —

EATING AND DRINKING

One fact of east European cooking in general is that it relies heavily on a meaty and starchy basis. One often thinks of Polish sausages, Hungarian goulash, and potatoes all around; throw in some cabbage sauerkraut and you've got the makings of a hearty peasant meal. Such traditional dishes have been handed down, and are still served today with a particular pride in the folk-country root and the image this inspires.

Czech food fits the description well. Typical dishes include generous portions of meat and either potatoes or special Czech dumplings, often laden with a thick sauce and washed down with a half-litre of beer or a glass of Moravian wine. In the most traditional pubs and restaurants, the setting is a smoky wood-panelled beer cellar, with red-checkered table cloths and possibly a grizzled old man playing accordion in a corner; a waiter in a dusty old tuxedo walks around the room with armfuls of beer mugs and steaming plates.

Though the sentimental value is one of its strong points, Czech food is the subject of much debate amongst foreign palates. Czechs for their part take enormous pride in visitors to the country who indulge themselves. Many first-timers indeed gush at the simple heartiness of it, soaking in the atmosphere with self-satisfied abandon. Connoisseurs of fine dining, meanwhile, cannot come to a consensus. Perhaps it's not surprising that Czech food hardly holds international status, compared with, say, French, Lebanese, or Japanese cuisine: maybe meat and potatoes isn't so refined after all. Although there is little overall variety in content or presentation, Czechs have developed many nuances in the standard offering.

The Carnivorous Czechs

If you're a meat lover you'll have a carnival indulging in the standard beef and pork fare, and at first you may feel like a kid who is suddenly free of the reins of your mother's insistence on a balanced diet. Czech cooking almost seems a conscious attempt to ignore nutritional advice and simply indulge in our predator-prey instinct. Imagine ordering a beefsteak topped with a slice of ham, a slice of cheese, and a fried egg; or try a deep-fat-fried pork chop with mashed potatoes swimming in a pool of butter. Some quip that the real purpose of Czech food is to line and fill the belly, for the sake of the beer that accompanies and follows the meal.

Czechs are indeed unabashed carnivores. Not only is meat the centrepiece to virtually any meal, it is additionally served as an ingredient in soups and salads, and you may easily eat more than one animal in more than one form at one single setting. The dietary habits are almost shocking. Not only are animal products the basis of most meals, the very preparation of the meals relies on excessive use of oil and lard for frying and in gravies. Vegetables are served almost as an afterthought.

One thing that makes Czech meat dishes exceptional and intriguing is the variety of sauces used, most of which contain very simple,

Beer, meat and music – the ingredients for a good time in the Czech Republic.

basic ingredients, yet lend a distinct flavour and edibility to them. There are many varieties of sauces and gravies poured over the meat: paprika, garlic, butter, and dill sauces are common, and each gives an enticing twist to what would otherwise be a monotonous offering. Plenty of potatoes and dumplings fill the plate, serving to soak up the gravy and balance the weight of the meat.

Healthy Fare

Those who appreciate more healthy fare may find it overwhelming at first, but dig around a bit and you'll learn how to cope. Traditional Czech fare has a strange aversion to fresh fruits and vegetables. Though they are sometimes present, their appearance is disguised in such a way that it seems they don't want to admit they're eating them. Most vegetables served in restaurants are either pickled or fried, even if they say it's fresh. The mushroom and cauliflower entrees (comprising the 'vegetarian' selection on the menu) are breaded and deep-fried. The cucumber salad you order is invariably going to be shredded and soaked in sugar-water, while the expected vegetable accompaniment to the entree is rarely more than a pickle or a piece of parsley. It can be frustrating. Chicken and fish are popularly consumed as something a bit 'lighter.'

Health-consciousness is finally kicking in, however, and you'll never really be in need. Soups are sturdy and wholesome; cabbage cream soup, for example, is delicious, and the special Czech version of potato soup is absolutely wonderful, with lots of onions and garlic. And of course, you are not limited to the standard offering in all restaurants: many places in fact have decent healthy dishes, and Prague has plenty of ethnic restaurants. There are always plenty of fresh fruit and vegetable stands around, and if you do your own cooking you'll have no problem obtaining the ingredients you want. It's up to you to be creative.

All in all, Czech food is hearty and delicious, though it may take some time to get used to. Many foreigners living in Prague comment that this was in fact the toughest thing to adjust to, though they immediately admit that it's not so bad – it's just easy to complain about. Some, this author for example, think quite highly of it.

THE DAILY MEALS

Even if the food is not particularly healthy or genteel, and you may come to think that Czechs somehow have different stomachs than others, they are keenly aware of body rhythms, and there are certain rules to when one should and should not take a meal. Breakfast *(snídaně)* is a quiet, reserved affair, perhaps because it's still dark for a good half the year as most people rise, but also because a hearty meal of eggs or doughnuts is considered too heavy in the morning – the body can't focus on the day's tasks when it is digesting. So breakfast tends to be little more than a cup of coffee, a piece of fruit, or yogurt.

Lunch *(oběd)* is often the main meal of the day, usually a bit more substantial than dinner unless one is specifically going out to eat in the evening. During the week, lunch is usually taken with colleagues and friends, and it is not a particularly drawn-out affair. Business-people and workers often go to a pub or office cafeteria for lunch, and children eat a full hot meal in the school canteen. The increasingly hectic work week now means that people are skipping or shortening their lunch breaks, and many are doing away with the formalities as they grab a sandwich when they find time. Lunchtime is generally between 11.30 am and 2.00 pm. On weekends, the family usually gathers for a meal prepared at home and served as the main meal of the day, at around one or two o'clock. This is normally a more relaxed affair than the Monday-Friday crunch, as everyone lounges around a bit, talking and watching TV.

The size and formality of the dinner *(večeře)* depends on whether it is enjoyed at home or in a restaurant, and on the whims of those who prepare it. Home meals are often simple, sometimes just a sausage, a bowl of soup, or even fruit filled dumplings, though sometimes dinner is a proper hot meal. When one goes out to dinner, the meal is a bit more relaxed than it is at lunch. Dinner is usually consumed no later than 7.30 or 8.00 pm; in fact many restaurants stop serving by nine o'clock.

The Order of the Meal

Your best and most likely place to mingle with the locals and eat traditional Czech food is in a pub or restaurant. The food typically served in these establishments is the same as that which is served at home, though due to Czechs' intensely private nature you aren't likely to be invited to friends' homes for dinner very often. Because of this, I've arranged the following section according to the menus you're likely to see when eating out.

Czechs don't give a lot of pretence to the meal itself. Lunch or dinner is rarely more than a soup and an entree, and when the food itself arrives it is often downed quickly. Conversation during the meal follows a similarly light-hearted trend. Deep discussion or playful argumentation on political or moralistic issues seem extraneous to the act of eating, a distraction to what should be a time of mental and physical relaxation. One therefore tends to speak about recent travels, plans for the weekend, a current film, or perhaps a problem in a relationship.

Note that restaurants occasionally 'run out' of selections, so think of a couple of options while making your choice.

Appetisers

Appetizers *(předkrm)* are in fact rarely ordered in restaurants nor are they served at home, as they are often quite heavy themselves. These are rather taken as snacks if you're stopping in for a drink, or as the meal itself if you're not very hungry.

Cheese platters *(sýrová mísa)* are common, and are composed of slices of Eidam cheese with a chunk of butter, a dash of paprika, and perhaps a pickle, and a basket of rolls. Meat platters are similar, though with slices of ham *(šunka)* or salami *(salám)* in addition to, or in place of, the cheese. A bit more substantial are the working-man's sausages available, from *párek* (bunless hot dogs) to *útopenec* (a thick pickled pink sausage) to *tlačenka* (animal parts in their own gel). *Utopenec* looks especially foul, brewing in big jars on the countertop, but I happen to like it. *Ďábelský toast* is a piquant ground beef mixture slopped on a slice of toast.

Soups

Although only a preview to the upcoming entree, Czech soups *(polévka)* are wonderful and in some cases are more the highlight. There are two basic types of soup: thick and hearty, and light and brothy.

The sturdy soups are almost a meal in themselves, with thick bases of flour and cream, and a few pungent spices to liven them up. Czech potato soup, called *bramborová polévka* though often referred to more intimately as *bramboračka*, is a marvellous concoction of

95

potatoes, carrots, dried mushrooms, and onions, with lots of garlic and marjoram. Once you've tried it you'll want to take the recipe home. Equally good is the cabbage cream soup *(zelná polévka)*, with a base of sauerkraut and milk or cream, pieces of sausage to bulk it up, and often flavoured with caraway seeds. Pea soup *(hráchová polévka)* is less common; when available it is a good split pea-and-ham type. White bean soup *(fazolová polévka)* is similar. Another Czech specialty is tripe (cow's stomach) soup, known as *dršt'ková*.

Soups of a brothy nature are also common and very good. Chicken and beef broths *(slepicí* and *hovězí vývar*, respectively) often have small pieces of meat, liver, and noodles in them. Even better though, are onion soup *(cibulová polévka*, or *cibulačka* for short) and garlic soup *(česneková polévka* or *česnečká)*, both often bulked up with pieces of potato and topped with croutons.

Salads

Most menus offer what they call fresh salads *(salát)*; in fact, very few of them are. Your best bet for a genuine fresh salad is *šopský salát*, a healthy mix of diced peppers, tomatoes, cucumbers, and onions in a watery dressing, with salty Balkan cheese (similar to Greek feta cheese) sprinkled on top. Except in the dead of winter, you can be sure of fresh ingredients. Likewise, the generic tossed *míchaný salát* is usually a fresh mixture of lettuce and a few pieces of tomato and cucumber. The danger here is that it often has a dollop of sauerkraut on top.

Other so-called salads are usually made of fresh vegetables, though they are mercilessly shredded and soaked in sweet vinegar water. These may appear as tomato *(rajčatový)*, cucumber *(okurkový)*, carrot *(mrkvový)*, or cabbage *(zelný)* salads.

Grocery stores and cheap eateries often have buckets of what they call salad in display cases. These are invariably cold, thick salads such as potato salad, egg salad, fish salad, and so on, all coagulated in mayonnaise. Some of the better places now offer decent salads of soya, pasta, rice, and vegetables.

Entrees/Main Courses

The heart and soul of Czech cooking lies in the hefty main course *(hlávní jídlo)* platter. Despite the lack of colour and variety, your eyes are bound to pop when they see that pile of meat and potatoes or dumplings. Home-cooked meals are a real treat, especially if you've grown accustomed to restaurant food.

Menus are often divided into types of meat, so you can better choose which type of beef, pork, chicken, or fish you'd like. Pubs usually have a list of ready-made dishes, such as goulash *(guláš)* and Wiener schnitzel *(vepřovy řízek)*, which come as a fixed plate with a side order included. Better pubs and restaurants prepare food to order.

The quintessential Czech dish is roast pork with flour dumplings and sauerkraut, whose proper name is affectionately shortened to *vepřo-knedlo-zelo*. It must be downed with a beer.

Goulash is a stew served on a plate, with lots of paprika sauce, pieces of onion or pickled red pepper on top, and flour dumplings to soak it all up. The meat is usually chunks of beef, sometimes with bits of fat still attached.

Another excellent dish is *svíčková* – beef sirloin, again with flour dumplings, and a flour gravy, topped with a piece of lemon and a spoonful of cranberry sauce.

There are many other cuts and preparations of meat, generally either roasted *(pečeně)* or fried *(smážený)*, and different establishments often have different names for and varieties of them. Look for the kinds of meat on offer, then decipher the menu to figure out how it is prepared and what sides and sauces accompany them. Common preparations include beef or pork steak *(steak* or *bíftek)*, roasts *(roštěná)*, and pounded schnitzel *(řízek)*.

Chicken is a popular product as well. Roast chicken *(kuře pečené)* is served with either potatoes or potato dumplings and topped with a succulent garlic sauce. You will likely find some form of fried chicken steak *(smážený kuřecí řízek)*, or grilled chicken *(kuřecí řízek)* sometimes with almonds and canned peaches or pineapple, as well.

Some establishments serve roast duck *(kachna)*, goose *(husa)*, and rabbit *(králík)*; these are delicacies here as anywhere.

Fish is very popular amongst Czechs, due to the large number of freshwater streams and the country's passion for fishing. Trout *(pstruh)* and carp *(kapr)* are the most common, either roasted or fried, and usually served with, again, potatoes or potato dumplings. Trout is the most common freshwater fish in the land, and it appears on many a dinner table. Czech carp is a little different from the bottom-dwelling fish in other parts of the world; it has a meaty texture and lots of tiny bones. Try it with garlic sauce *(kapr na česneku)* – it's excellent.

Vegetarian Entrees (bezmasa or vegeterianské jídlo)

Yes, there are meatless dishes to be ordered too. One of the most popular is fried cheese *(smážený sýr)*, a thick slice of Eidam or Hermelin cheese, breaded and deep-fat-fried. It's sinfully rich and unhealthy, especially when taken with *pommes-frites* (chips, fries), and it's usually served with tartar sauce. Wonderful. Be sure to eat it quickly, while the cheese is still runny.

Fried mushrooms *(smážené žampiony)* and fried cauliflower *(smažený květák)* are the other options here, again breaded and deep-fried. Lentils *(čočky)* are often available, usually served in huge proportions with a fried egg resting on top.

Sides (příloha)

Czech dumplings (*knedlíky*) are a matter of national pride. They're quite unlike the dumplings one normally comes across, and in fact you may not even recognise them as such when you first see them. There are two types, flour dumplings *(houskový knedlík)* and potato dumplings *(bramborový knedlík)*; both are boiled as round loaves and sliced into thick chunks. You'll be served three or four of them to soak up the sauce on your plate. There are a few varieties of dumplings, for example *spičkový knedlík* have bits of bacon mixed into the batter, and there are apparently subtle distinctions in quality which any blue-blooded Czech will quickly determine. The home-made ones are always the best, and most people scoff at the store bought mixes available – such things require special attention. Perhaps because Czechs are so proud of their *knedlíky*, foreigners are quick to ridicule what appears to be little more than boiled bread, though most agree they have their merits. When eating those thick dumplings, one slops sauce on top of the bready substance with the knife and carefully raises it to the mouth.

Potatoes come in the usual styles, boiled *(vářené)*, mashed *(kaše)*, or as chips or fries *(hranolky)*, though they are in fact of uniformly inferior quality to the assortment of potatoes eaten in many other countries. Rice *(ryže)* and pasta *(těstoviny)* are less common.

Side orders are sometimes included as part of the menu offering; if not, they will be listed at the end of the menu and are not included in the price.

Desserts *(moučníky)*

Desserts *(moučníky or dezerty)* are always included in restaurant menus, and are occasionally served at home, though Czechs rarely indulge in more than coffee after the main course. In fact, your waiter will probably not ask if you want a dessert, so you'll have to request the menu again if you do. Keep in mind that desserts are often just as heavy as the food that came before it, so save some room. There are a few particular ones which you must try.

The king of sweets in this land is the fabulous fruit-filled dumpling *(ovocný knedlík)*. Large round flour dumplings are filled with plums or apricots, dripped with butter, and sprinkled with curd. Coming after an already heavy meal, this is the height of gluttony, though you really must try it.

Another popular dessert is light crepes, known as *palačinky*, rolled up and filled with jam, and occasionally topped with whipped cream.

Ice cream *(zmrzlina)* is more commonly bought on the street from a vendor, though some type of ice cream sundae is usually available in restaurants. It is often topped with canned fruit *(kompot)*, though sometimes they pour chocolate on top of that, with little regard for clashing tastes. Oh well.

Drinks (Nápoje)

Beer and wine accompany the meal, though if you abstain you can always order a cola *(kola)*, mineral or soda water *(mineralka* or *sodovka)*, tea *(čaj)*, or coffee *(káva)*. Beware of *džus*, pronounced and intended to be 'juice.' Unless it specifically states that it is 100% juice, it will be a powder-mix neon-orange sugar water.

SNACKS

Czechs consume lots of meaty snacks at all times of the day, often stopping at a street stand to pick up a sausage or a roll. You'll never be far from a counter from which you can buy a hot dog wrapped in a bun *(párek v rohlíku)*. Stands up and down Wenceslas Square in Prague serve thick hearty sausages *(klobása)*, accompanied by a hunk of bread and a dollop of mustard on a paper tray. You're meant to eat it with your hands. Cheap pubs serve it too – this is the mainstay of many. Greasy potato pancakes *(bramborák)* are made of shredded potatoes and lots of garlic fried in lard – a nightmare for the arteries and breath, but a tasty treat nonetheless.

Lunch spots and grocery stores often have an extensive selection of small, open-faced sandwiches called *chlebíčky*. Three or four of these could make a poor-man's lunch. These usually have a layer of potato salad topped with ham, salami, egg, cheese, or fish, and a garnish of pickle, onion, or parsley. There's usually an additional dollop of mayonnaise as well. It makes for a tall mouthful: don't attempt to eat one while walking, or you'll get it all down your shirt. *Chlebíčky* in fact are considered a delicacy, even if more refined cultures may scoff at the baseness of it – you'll likely see them offered at balls and during intermission at the symphony.

Sweet snacks are eaten regularly as well. Ice cream is immensely popular in warm weather, and street stands across the country have lines of people forming to indulge in small cones with minuscule scoops of merely average ice cream. The quintessential Czech pastry is the *koláč*, a round sweetbread carved out at the top and filled with curd, poppy seeds, or fruity paste; it looks almost like a mini-pizza.

SEASONAL SPECIALTIES

There are a few seasonal specialties to spice up the usual offerings. These for the most part are consumed at home, though good restaurants may play their part and serve the following as well.

Within a week or two at the end of April or beginning of May, everyone opens their windows, and a funny thing happens: people start eating fresh fruits and vegetables again! It's almost as if the seasons dictate the diet, and while it's normal to eat pickles and sauerkraut for six months, all of a sudden it's part of the celebration of spring to eat fresh oranges, tomatoes, and peppers again. So refreshing!

Fall is the traditional harvest time, and there are a few culinary pleasures to be discovered. As mushrooms pop up in the forests, people head out with wicker baskets to pick them – and these aren't just regular mushrooms. Czechs have a sharp eye for fungi, and they quickly fill up on monstrous beautiful creations recalling images of *Alice in Wonderland*. These are then taken home where they are dried, fried, or put into thick soups. At around the same time, many villagers perform an almost ritual pig slaughter, called *zabíjačka*. The poor beast is strung up by its haunches and gutted, and all body parts are used to make chops, sausages, and goulash.

Christmas of course has a traditional meal, but the surprise here is that the dish is not meat based. Throughout November and December, the carp ponds of south Bohemia are harvested and the chunky foot-long fish are wheeled into town in large barrels, where they are sold live. The faithful take them home and let them swim in the bathtub until the 24th, when the fish are fried up and served next to a bed of cold potato salad. I always thought this was summer food, but the custom on Christmas day is delightful.

DRINKING
Beer

Beer *(pivo)* is the pride, joy, and ritual passion of the Czech people. Czechs were in fact one of the very first nations to brew and drink beer. The word 'pilsner' itself comes down to us from the Czech beer-producing town of Plzeň, which is recorded as selling a famous malty lager brew in 1307. So devoted were the city's inhabitants that they rioted when the recipe was subsequently altered. Plzeň is still home to some of the country's (and hence the world's) finest brands, Pilsner Urquell and Gambrinus. Pilsner Urquell (Plzeňsky Prazdroj in Czech) became so popular after its founding in 1842 that it spawned a series of German imitations (the Czech lands were heavily populated by Germans at this time), marketed under the type name 'pilsner.' The company then had to add the qualifier *urquell* in German, and *prazdroj* in Czech (source), to identify it as the original. Great German beers thus owe a tip of the hat to the Czechs for setting them on the right track in this regard.

Another beer word you're probably familiar with is Budweiser, whose name is taken from Budweis, the German name for the south Bohemian city of České Budějovice. Not only the Germans, but also the Americans have exploited this name for their own weak imitations. The American company Anheuser-Busch is currently embroiled in a long-running dispute with the Budějovicky Budvar brewery over the international trademark, to such an extent that the Americans would like to buy a majority share in the Czech label – either to get their product here or to keep the vastly better Czech brand out of the States. Fortunately for connoisseurs, it doesn't look like it will happen.

Czech advertisers have come up with some clever eye-grabbers expounding the local adulation. One popular ad for Staropramen beer shows a classic smoky old beer hall with bearded men worshipping at the table, chanting *Bud' pochválen* ("be praised") while the waiters pour the loving nectar in slow motion. One beer's slogan is *Dej Bùh štěstí* ("God gives happiness"); Pilsner Urquell plays on its own name, selling itself as *Prazdroj naše hrdost* – "the source of our pride." Little wonder then that Czechs consume far greater quantities of beer per capita than anyone else in the world.

The drink itself is indeed honourable: full-bodied, foamy, and fit for a king. Hops growing is an art form, and a jaunt into parts of north and west Bohemia will lead you through massive wooden hops frames filling the fields. It is not really known why, but Bohemian hops simply produces the best beer, and in fact it is exported to many foreign manufacturers. Domestic brewers say it is simply the method used and the care given to the brewing that produces such a fine drink.

Czech beer is not produced in such varieties as elsewhere. There are two kinds, light and dark, and there are different grade strengths within each. Variations such as bitter, white, amber, or fruity beers, as available in countries such as Britain, Germany, and Belgium, are not considered 'real' beer by Czech connoisseurs.

Proper Czech beer is a golden lager brew, commonly referred to as 'light' *(světlé)*, though not at all to be mistaken for the low-calorie stuff. It is invariably well toned, and comes in two strengths – 10° *(desítka)* and 12° *(dvanáctka)*. These do not indicate percentages of alcohol but grades of sugar content. The heavier the degree of sugar, however, the stronger the beer. Ten-degree beer is lighter in colour, often sweeter, and contains about 3-4% alcohol. Regular pub-goers often prefer it because the stomach can process more of it during a lengthy drinking session. Twelve-degree beer is stronger and heavier – it normally contains about 4-4.5% alcohol – with a thick golden-brown colour and frothy foam that doesn't want to go down. In fact it is said that the best way to judge a good beer is if a wooden matchstick, placed vertically in the head, stays afloat for more than ten seconds. If you intend to really go out drinking, moderate your intake of 12° beer; even life-long veterans can wake up with a vicious headache if they down more than four or five.

Dark, or 'black' beer *(tmávé or černé)* is indeed almost black, and often very sweet – many drinkers find it too sugary. For this reason it is less commonly drunk than regular beers, though it is often mixed with light beer and referred to as *řezáné*, literally 'cut' beer.

The best place to consume is in the pub, where beer is poured fresh from the tap. Most pubs only offer one brand of beer, some offering both the 10° and 12° varieties. Bottled beer is available everywhere, most shops offering a greater selection than the one brand served at the corner pub. You may soon develop your favourite brands, though for the most part each is similar enough and good enough that beginners won't easily distinguish between them.

Beer is traditionally served in sturdy half-litre glass mugs, or sometimes in large tall glasses. Czechs sometimes order a small *(malé)* beer at lunch and when they only want a taste. As much as they enjoy their national claim to fame, though, they tend to swallow it in gulps rather than sip it gracefully.

The Major Labels

While there are several major labels, marketing their product across the land and abroad, there are dozens of local brands as well, and a trip to any town out of Prague should include a sampling of the local product. Most pubs in Prague and many around the country serve one of the following:

- **Pilsner Urquell** (referred to by regular drinkers as simply *Plzeň*), is the export leader, with the green and white label familiar to most educated beer drinkers around the world. This is one of the country's, and the world's, premier brands. Most pubs that serve it serve the 12° brew, which is particularly excellent.

- **Gambrinus**, also brewed in Plzeň, is similarly top-of-the-line – the 12° variety is arguably the very best in the land.

- **Budvar**, the original Czech 'Budweiser' is at least as good as Pilsner Urquell and Gambrinus, though unfortunately less widely available. Again, the 12° is preferred over the 10°.

- **Krušovické** is a small brewery in western Bohemia, producing a slightly more pale lager with a faintly metallic-bitter aftertaste. A fresh 12° Krušovické poured from a friendly tap is my personal favourite.

- **Velkopopovicky Kozel**, produced just south of Prague, also has good 12° beers, though they've drawn some criticism for their sexy ad campaigns, which make a pun of their name: *kozel* means goat, and the creature is indeed used on the brand's label, though the word is also dangerously similar to that for breast.

- **Radegast**, from Ostrava in Moravia, makes fine 10° and 12° beers.

- **Regent**, from Třeboň in south Bohemia, has a slightly sweet, light beer.

- **Staropramen** is Prague´s main producer, with a large brewery on the banks of the Vltava in Smíchov. This is working-man's beer;

the 10° vies with Radegast for the annual 'best Czech beer' award, though the 12° is also quite good.

- **Branické** and **Měšt'án** are smaller Prague breweries, both producing decent lagers. Měšt'án makes one of the best dark beers in the country.

- **Purkmistr** also produces a fine dark beer.

WINE

It's often commented that Bohemians are enthusiastic beer-guzzlers, while Moravians are slightly more refined aficionados of their wine. South Moravia indeed is an endless stretch of vineyards, and its red and white wines are enjoyed throughout the country. Although it doesn't quite match up to fine French vintages, Moravian wine is still very drinkable and goes well with certain foods.

The wine drinking establishment is a common gathering place, admittedly more reserved and genteel than the pub, and usually offering a slightly more sophisticated ambience for a quiet dinner. Wine is often sold right out of the barrel at wine bars *(vinárna)*; if you bring your own bottle you can walk off with a good, fresh, yet inexpensive brand.

The chief wine-producing regions are around the towns of Znojmo and Mikulov in south Moravia, though there are also respectable wines bottled in north Bohemia around Mělník. Seasonal festivals celebrate the harvest and fermentation of local wines. In October, wine-producing regions erupt in jolly *burčák*, or "young wine" festivals. The honoured drink is an extremely fruity liquid, very cloudy in appearance and almost indiscernible from plain old grape juice in taste. This, of course, is part of the popularity of it: the alcohol is so masked by the fresh flavour that you don't even realise how much you've drunk before it's too late! Be forewarned.

In the wintertime hot mulled wine *(svařené víno)* is a popular balm. Red wine is boiled with stick cinnamon and cloves, and sweetened with sugar. The cosiest sensations of winter involve strolling the Christmas stalls with a cup of hot wine, or relaxing in a snowbound cottage with friends and plenty of mugs.

Champagne *(šampán or sekt)* is drunk at special occasions, and there are a few reasonable local brands. Russian champagne is also quite popular, while French champagne is still beyond the budget of many and not well known.

Red Wines

Frankovka is a dry, full-flavoured wine, produced by many domestic vineyards. *Vavřinecké* is a bit sweeter and smoother.

White Wines

Ryzlink is a semi-dry, neutral wine, a good accompaniment to fish dishes. Müller-Thurgau is a bit sweeter, and is the most commonly produced white wine in the country.

OTHER ALCOHOLIC DRINKS

Czechs are proud possessors of a special herb liquor called *Becherovka*. This drink is difficult to describe, quite unlike anything else of its ilk. The ingredients in fact are a well protected secret – the recipe is literally locked safely away, and only one person is entitled to blend the concoction. Its most immediately recognisable components are chamomile and cloves; if you have a highly distinguished palate you may be able to identify more.

Becherovka is made in the spa town of Karlovy Vary (Karlsbad), where it was created as an additional salve for patients who spent their days imbibing mineral water, soaking in steam baths, and walking in the fresh air. Because of this, it is reputed to have medicinal properties. A little drink after work is said to calm the nerves in a more wholesome way than say, scotch, and when taken as an aperitif it is said to aid in digestion. Some even use it liberally to cure colds.

Slivovice *(slivovitz)* is another local specialty, produced and drunk more in Moravia and Slovakia, from whence it comes. This is powerful stuff – clear, distilled from plums and served in tiny shot glasses. It is also purported to have medicinal qualities, though to be swallowed in strict moderation. Similar schnapps-type drinks are distilled from apricots *(meruňkovice)* and cherries *(třešňovice)*, though these have a sickly sweet nature that makes them almost unpalatable. You also occasionally see folks throwing back shots of fluorescent green peppermint liqueur; not very appetising.

Rum is popular in wintertime, especially when poured into a cup of hot water and garnished with a lemon, called *grog*. Czech rum is distilled from sugarbeets, not sugarcane, and therefore has a dark brown colour and powerfully sweet flavour. I personally can't drink it. Equally bad in my opinion is Fernet, an even darker brown, a thick aperitif whose ingredients are a secret, and therefore are said to include fermented bugs. Vodka and gin are also produced locally, though their quality pales in comparison to their international counterparts.

Many people are now enjoying drinks that were strictly black market specialties under Communism, such as whiskey and tequila.

COFFEE AND TEA

Czechs truly enjoy a quiet cup of coffee *(káva)*. The brown bean is said to have made its way to Bohemia via Turkish traders in the 16th century, and since then has been an important component of the daily diet. Perhaps falling back on such tradition, Czech coffee is usually served 'Turkish-style,' with boiling water poured directly over finely ground beans. This lends it a decidedly rich, silty effect. Stir it well, and let the grounds settle to the bottom – and when you get to the bottom of the cup, be sure not to swallow the last mouthful or you'll get a throat full of mud.

The custom seems frozen in time, and sitting in one of Prague's formerly glorious coffee houses gives the sensation of being transported back to the 1930s. Czechs claim that they have always had the best coffee – even under Communism, they had it shipped specially from Cuba. To be honest, it's not at all bad, but there's nothing particularly enticing about it. Most people add sugar, though milk is usually left out.

Coffee-machine coffee *(presso)* is also widely available, though you'll have to clarify that you'd prefer it to the Turkish-style. Many upscale places are abandoning their old ways altogether: Westerners drink filtered coffee, so Turkish is becoming passé. Italians and other connoisseurs please note that the espresso and cappuccino you see on many menus is rarely as good as you may expect.

Special preparations of coffee add excitement to the pleasure of drinking it, especially in cold weather. *Vídeňská* (Viennese) coffee is a robust blend topped with whipped cream, served in an appropriately elegant handled glass. Even more heartwarming is *Alžirská* (Algerian), with a drop of egg liqueur atop the whipped cream.

Tea has unfortunately never been an important drink in these parts. Czech tea is pretty bland stuff, though foreign made brands are now widely available. It is usually served black, with lemon and sugar. Fruit teas and herb teas are now becoming popular, and Prague has several excellent tea shops with a relaxed atmosphere and wonderful selection of international blends.

WATER

In a land famous for its spas, mineral water is excellent and widely drunk. In addition to the beer and Becherovka produced here, a particular brand of mineral water called Mattoni completes the trinity of special, top quality drinks. This is a wonderfully fine, slightly fizzy water with a light, refreshing taste, served in many restaurants and sold in most shops. Soda water is always available. Non-carbonated (still) water is only sold in shops – Dobrá Voda is far and away the market leader here and tap water is never served in restaurants nor drunk at home. Tap water is in fact drinkable – there are no especially harmful elements therein – but it can taste pretty foul.

EATING AND DRINKING OUT: PUBS AND RESTAURANTS

The basic drinking establishment in the Czech Republic is the pub, and there are subtle differences between the types of pubs and the drinks and food they offer. The very word of course implies beer, and many pubs exist for the sole purpose of pouring half-litres of the foamy stuff. A *hospoda* is your basic pub, serving beer on tap, bottled wine, and an assortment of liquors. A *hospoda* normally serves a variety of prepared meals. A *hostinec* or *pivnice* is a simpler and more intimate version of a *hospoda*, with a more limited food offering; some in fact have only bags of potato chips (crisps) and maybe a sausage. Pubs usually serve only one brand of beer, and many pubs are named or referred to simply for the beer they serve.

Another interpretation to the idealised vision of a traditional pub mentioned in the previous section is the general dirtiness of many: crowded, noisy, smoke filled rooms with dirty tablecloths, and waiters mumbling and shuffling about, which is the norm in the cheaper joints. Glasses aren't always properly washed: every bar has a sink full of water into which glasses are dunked, swished around, and stacked to dry. Drunken patrons who spend every evening of their lives at the same table unfurl occasional shouts. It's all quite funny, and all it takes is just a little lightening up and hunkering down to fit in.

Restaurace are categorized as proper restaurants, though the difference between a good *hospoda* and a cheap *restaurace* is nominal. The original sense of the word 'restaurant' implies food, while 'pub' implies beer, and because of this, *restaurace* generally have a better variety and quality of food.

Lower end pubs and restaurants serve cheap, albeit greasy meals. A goulash and a beer for lunch at such a place shouldn't run you more than US$3 or so. Keep in mind when choosing a place to eat that Czechs are avid smokers; nonsmoking sections are unheard of, ventilation is poor, and in most pubs you'll be overwhelmed by a blast of hazy blue-grey smoke when you enter.

Moving up the scale, better restaurants pay closer attention to food preparation. The difference between a goulash thrown together at a cheap joint, and one prepared with a careful blend of seasonings at a respectable restaurant, can be substantial. So where you might be driven away by the idea of Czech food from a cheap pub, you'll gain a real appreciation for the specialised art of Czech cuisine at a good restaurant. For this you'll pay something closer to Western standards, though still cheap in comparison, say US$15–20 per person for a full meal with drinks.

Ethnic foods are becoming increasingly popular. Prague especially is full of pizzerias and Mexican, Irish, Chinese, Lebanese, and American restaurants dot the city's streets, many of them run by expatriates. You'll undoubtedly seek refuge in the variety and the vegetables they serve. Pizzerias generally charge from $3–6 for a large personal thin crust pizza. A meal at a Chinese or Tex-Mex restaurant will run about $10–15, while a fine French or Japanese restaurant will cost about what you would expect anywhere. Please note: if you want ethnic food, don't look for it at a Czech restaurant. Though lots of places now serve 'Chinese meat' or 'Milanese spaghetti,' it will most certainly be a poor imitation.

All eating and drinking establishments are classified by price, and by law this rating must be posted on the door or above the bar. A class IV pub is the dirtiest and cheapest, a class III pub is generally reasonable, a class II pub or restaurant is of good to excellent quality, while class I restaurants are the most exclusive. The Communists started this practice to insure that the price of a meal will be exactly the same in Prague as in Pelhřimov, and though the market has now changed, the system is still in place. Not only did the Communists regulate the prices, they also monotonised the substance in question. All chefs had to pass certain courses in food preparation, and all were required to follow a book of guidelines as to how each dish can be prepared. With no room for creativity, Czech food became even more predictable than it is already was.

Pub Culture

Because of the inherent difference in standards between a cheap pub and a good restaurant, there are different (unwritten) rules for behaviour in them. Where service in a good restaurant is similar to what you would expect anywhere, pubs are a bit rougher and it helps to understand the mentality so as not to upset anyone. Here are a few dos and don'ts of drinking out.

Waiters and waitresses in pubs are generally inattentive, though customer service is slowly becoming a part of the Czech vocabulary. The main reason for this is that they are underpaid, they don't receive tips, and therefore they have no incentive. At the same time, the waiter is on a power trip; this is his domain and you'd best respect it. Be patient. Don't attempt to draw attention to yourself by signalling the waiter; he'll come to you in his own time.

In most restaurants and pubs you are expected to seat yourself. Pubs rarely have tables for two – patrons tend to sprawl out along the bench-like tables, and it's perfectly normal to share a table with someone you don't know. In fact, this is often your only option. If you see free space at the end of a table, ask with the appropriate hand

A Typical Czech pub – focus of much of the social activity in the country.

motions if the spot is free, and seat yourself. Do not, however, move chairs around without first consulting the server. Remember, you are in his house!

Most establishments have coat racks; it is a bit lower-class to drape your jacket over the back of your seat, even in a regular pub. Better restaurants have cloakrooms, where you often pay 2 Kč to hang your bags and coats. Many older citizens often dress up a bit when they go out. As pubs are still the central focus of Czech social life, a tradition remains of respecting the institution. Casual dress and jeans are perfectly acceptable, of course, and only very rarely will a restaurant look down their nose at you for being under-dressed.

In the real pubs, you rarely need to order beer, as it is simply plopped down in front of you – after all, isn't this why you came? Your waiter will place a tab on the table, with lines to indicate the number of beers consumed. A glance at your neighbour's tab may well reveal a whole slur of lines; if you really want to integrate you can try to play catch-up. Don't by any means write on or rip your tab – it can potentially cause confusion when adding it all up in the end.

Always toast your friends before taking your first swallow of the evening, and always look into your companion's eyes when doing so. This is part of the ritual of drinking. Never pour beer from one glass to another: the half-litre is sacred, and you may draw a few harsh stares if you don't so honour it.

One curiosity of eating in a pub is that it can take a while to place your order and get someone to come and add up the bill, though for some reason your plate seems to be whisked away the moment you lay down your fork.

Paying the bill often seems to take a long time. Often the person who collects your money is different from the one who has served you. When you're ready to go, say to your waiter or the person with the money purse, *zaplatíme* ("we will pay"). He will then invariably ask, *dohromady?* ("altogether?"), hoping to save himself extra work, though it is fine to pay separately (*zvlášt'*). When your dining or drinking companion is on even keel with you, this is common enough, though if someone does the inviting or otherwise feels obliged, he often takes the tab himself. You as a visitor will probably have difficulty trying to pay, as your friends and colleagues will perpetually want to welcome you. Credit cards are rarely accepted in the lower end and non-touristed establishments, so have cash on hand.

Rip-offs do occur. It's gotten much better since the early 1990s, when foreigners were hapless prey to greedy waiters; it is unlikely that you'll be cheated now, but be sure to verify the prices and the final addition. As the calculations are done right there at the table, there is potential for honest mistakes to be made, though it is considered pretty bad form to check the bill's final count unless you're sure that something is amiss.

Tipping is limited to rounding up the tab to the nearest reasonable figure. The person who takes your money may not be your waiter, anyway, so he doesn't deserve any particular tip. If you have a beer tab for 92 Kč, round it up to 100 Kč and the guy will thank you. If your meal comes to 335 Kč, round up to 350 Kč. Better restaurants, especially foreign owned ones, expect higher tips, but it is still nowhere near the 15% expected in some parts of the world. Such roundups are always done on the spot: when the waiter tells you the amount, tell him how much you would like to pay. Never leave money on the table; it will be snatched up by the next guy who sits there.

Remember that many pubs and restaurants close as early as 10:00 or 11:00 pm.

Chapter Seven

DAILY NECESSITIES

SHOPPING

Under 41 years of Communist rule, shopping in the Czech Republic was a torturous rigamarole to be avoided unless absolutely necessary. It's not that there weren't any goods or that there weren't enough of them, it's just that obtaining them was a Herculean endeavour. The grocery store that carried your favourite yogurt one day didn't have it the next; the selection of trousers offered by the department store was uniformly cheap; the service anywhere you went was almost purposefully savage. In a society not kind to materialism, you were supposed to be grateful for what you got.

All that has changed since 1989, and the quality and availability of everything from light bulbs to salmon steaks has improved beyond measure. This has been achieved partly through foreign establishments – department stores were snatched up by firms such as K-mart and Krone, while clothing shops such as Benetton and supermarket chains such as Delvita set up and began to run a brisk trade. The products available in these and all the newly opened Czech-owned shops have brought great variety to the shelves. The increasingly competitive market has also forced Czech manufacturers to improve their products, and they have often done this while keeping retail prices lower than the imports, so the act of shopping becomes more and more interesting.

Prague is not a place one would think of to come to on a shopping spree, however, and it probably never will be. Prices of imported goods are at least as high here as anywhere else, and local products for the most part simply don't hold up to international standards, though they are often significantly cheaper. You will have fun poking into craft shops and through Christmas stalls, where traditional Czech things such as world famous Bohemia crystal, wooden puppets, and lace make great gifts and home decorations. If you've got time to kill, Prague can be a good place to explore newly opened specialty boutiques, as well as antique markets and flea markets.

For your standard, day-to-day shopping needs, you'll likely build a memory bank of a few places that consistently have what you're looking for, and return to these places when necessary. I limit my shopping to the essentials, and I stick with large department stores or specific shops that I know to avoid potential frustrations.

FOOD SHOPPING
Grocery Stores
Food shopping is usually done at small, local grocery stores called *potraviny*. Czechs often pick up the daily essentials at the *potraviny* around the corner, rather than in an American style weeks-worth trip to the supermarket. Changing work patterns are having an impact on this custom, however. *Potraviny* are generally quite small and crowded, and stock the essentials: frozen meat and vegetables, canned goods, dairy products, fresh bread and rolls, bottled and boxed drinks, sweets, soup mixes, spices, alcohol, and often a mini-delicatessen with pickled salads and fresh cold cuts and cheese. Most also have a bottle return counter – be sure to save all glass bottles and return them for a 3 Kč return on your deposit.

Potraviny and supermarkets now stock both domestic and imported brands, though you may have no choice in the matter. You will recognise many brands such as Coca-Cola, Heinz, and Uncle Ben's next to the local equivalent (often at double the price). Don't be afraid to go local – quality is generally as good, and sometimes better. Some international brands in fact manufacture their goods in the Czech Republic, making them competitively priced against the humbler local products.

One custom to be aware of in all grocery stores is that you must have a shopping cart or basket to enter the shop, even if you're just picking up a pack of cigarettes from the check-out counter. Shopping carts sometimes require a deposit of a 10 Kč coin, which you insert into the slot on the cart. The practical reason for this is to keep all the carts in one neat place at the entrance. During busy hours there are sometimes lines in front of the check-out counter of people waiting to get baskets and carts from paying customers, just to get into the store! Some *potraviny* employ a highly inefficient system of keeping all groceries behind the counter – you have to just wait in line and have the shop assistant get everything for you.

Plastic bags are rarely offered, you must ask for one specifically and will probably have to pay 2 Kč or so for it. Most people bring their own bags with them. You are expected to bag your own groceries, so a time-saving trick is to start bagging while the check-out person is ringing up the tab.

Fruits and Vegetables

Potraviny don't normally carry much in the way of fresh fruits and vegetables, though they do have shelves and shelves of items such as stewed fruit, pickles, pickled carrots, pickled peppers, and pickled cabbage.

For a better selection, find an *ovoce-zelenina* shop (greengrocer's) or an outdoor fruit and vegetable stand. Hardy local fruits and vegetables, such as apples, pears, potatoes, carrots, and cabbage, are always available; others such as tomatoes and bell peppers are usually available as well, though as anywhere, are cheapest and best in-season. A lot of fresh produce is now imported and you can almost always get oranges, bananas, and the like at most produce vendors. Even 'exotic' foods such aubergines, broccoli, and mangoes are sometimes available.

In Prague, the best selection of fresh produce is at the Havelská *tržiště* (market), on Havelská street between Wenceslas Square and Old Town Square. For hard-to-get produce such as sweet potatoes or cilantro, a shop called Fruits de France, on Jindříšská street near Wenceslas Square, will be a life-saver.

While it's common to ask for, say, two bananas, or five onions, most fresh produce is purchased by weight. If you're unfamiliar with the metric system, this is a good opportunity to learn it.

Useful Words

- *jablko* – apple
- *pomeranč* – orange
- *banán* – banana

- *hruška* – pear
- *švestka* – plum
- *mandarinka* – mandarins
- *hroznové víno* – grapes
- *ananas* – pineapple
- *brusinky* – cranberries
- *fazole* – bean

- *brambor* – potato
- *mrkev* – carrot
- *paprika* – bell pepper (In summer these are light green and hot.)
- *cibule* – onion
- *rajče*—tomatoes
- *zelí* – cabbage/sauerkraut
- *květák* – cauliflower
- *houba* or *žampion* – mushroom
- *hrašek* – pea

Meat, Poultry, Fish, and Cheeses

While *potraviny* and supermarkets always have a decent selection of meats, whether fresh-packaged or frozen, the best fresh meats are to be found at a butcher's shop *(řeznictví)*. These usually have signs outside saying simply *maso-úzeniny*, and generally stick to beef and

119

pork products. You can order special cuts of meat and sausage by weight (it is normally requested in decigrams or in half or whole kilogram quantities).

Note that the methods of butchering meat are somewhat different from what you may be used to; a good solid T-bone steak, for example, is hard to find. Ground beef is rarely out on the shelves, but can be requested (ask for *mleté hovězí.*) Cold cuts are also quite common, packaged or sliced at the deli; there are several different types of hams and salamis available.

For the freshest fish and poultry, head to a *ryby-drůbež* shop, where the fish are sometimes still swimming in the tank. The procedure is the same as in the *řeznictví:* ask for specific cuts by weight. Czechs eat a lot of beef and pork, and therefore fish and poultry shops are less common.

Useful Words

- *hovězí* – beef
- *vepřova* – pork
- *játra* – liver
- *kuře* – chicken
- *šunka* – ham
- *husa* – goose
- *kachna* – duck
- *ryba* – fish
- *kapr* – Czech carp
- *pstruh* – trout
- *turistický, poličan, lovecký* and *úherský* are basic salamis
- *párek* and *klobása* are sausages.

Cheeses are available in wide variety at *potraviny*, though many butcheries offer good selections as well. Aside from the soft, spreadable cheeses *(távenný syr)* so popular here, hard cheeses are common, whether packaged on the shelf or cut for you at the counter.

Useful Words

- *eidam-* – Czech variety of the Dutch eidam
- *zlato* – soft, pungent yellow-white cheese
- *hermelín* – a cheap camembert
- *úzený sýr* – smoked cheese

Bread and Pastries

The best place to buy fresh bread is at a bakery *(pekářství)*. The most commonly seen grains are *chléb* (always spoken of as *chleba),* a thick heavy rye variety loaf, which you can buy whole, halved, or quartered; and *rohlíky* and *housky*, tasty white rolls of mini-baguette and braided roll variety, respectively.

Other types of bread, such as pita *(Arabsky chléb)*, graham and various whole-grains can be found in bakeries, as can a long line of pastries. The most common are *koláč*, a flat sweet bread with fruit, cream or poppy seed toppings; *koblíha*, jelly doughnuts; and *závin*, apple strudel.

Supermarkets

There are now several Western-style supermarkets around the country, stocking everything you would find in your supermarket at home. These are smaller than the American-style grocery store warehouses, but still are adequate. Prague has several excellent supermarkets in the basements of many central department stores, including Tesco, Krone, and Kotva.

Toiletries and Pharmaceuticals

Potraviny often carry a supply of soap, dish detergent, toothpaste, shaving cream, and toilet paper, though you might have to go to yet another shop for these. *Drogerie* are, despite the name, shops that carry such personal items.

As with food, Czech toiletries are of good-enough quality, though you don't have the variety or top quality available at home. You can find recognisable brands in most places you look. The only toiletry item you may have trouble obtaining is deodorant – local deodorants are usually heavily perfumed sprays, and Czechs aren't quite as fastidious about scenting the armpits as others. I always pick up a Speed Stick to bring back when I'm in the States.

Pharmaceuticals, including both prescription and over-the-counter drugs, are sold exclusively at a *lékárna*. Even aspirin and cold medicine can only be bought at a *lékárna*, though these are located all over town. Look for the green sign with the familiar snake-shield logo. Note that many of the over-the-counter drugs you may be accustomed to buying at home are considered prescription medications here (see section on Health).

Useful Words

- *toalitní papír* – toilet paper (This is often cardboard-like and uncomfortable.)
- *papírové kapesníky* – facial tissues (Mini-packets of tissues are available, though most Czechs use cloth handkerchiefs.)
- *holící krém* – shaving cream
- *žiletky* – razor blades
- *mydlo* – soap
- *šampon*—shampoo
- *vlasový kondicioner* – hair conditioner
- *pěna do koupele* – bubble bath
- *krém* – body lotion
- *zubní pasta* – toothpaste
- *vložky* or *tampon* – tampon
- *prezervativ* or *kondom* – condom

Paper towels are tough to find other than at Western shops like Tesco.

CLOTHES

Unfortunately Czech clothing is nothing to shout about. It's not particularly bad, but then it's not particularly good either. Prices are quite a bit lower than the glamour international names, and if you're not too fastidious, the quality is good enough. One friend who has lived here for four years says that finding good quality, reasonably priced clothes is one of her greatest frustrations. She, like many, prefers to supply her wardrobe from home.

Nevertheless, you can easily find shirts, trousers, sweaters, jackets, dresses, undergarments, socks, and shoes. Large department stores *(obchodní dům)* in many cities stock general clothing needs, and offer both domestic and foreign brands. Small specialized boutiques *(obchod)* flood Prague's centre, selling well known brands such as Levi's, Hugo Boss, Stefanel, Benetton, Reporter, and many more. These are the best places to buy casual dress clothes and business attire.

Street vendors also sell clothes, though the quality is often dubious. Finally, second-hand shops *(second hand* or *levné zboží)* are common and well used, and offer a surprisingly good collection of decent clothes.

Useful Words

- *košile* – button-down shirt
- *mikina* – pullover sweat-shirts
- *tričko* – T-shirt
- *svetr* – sweater
- *sako* – dress jacket, blazer
- *kalhoty* – trousers
- *šaty* – dress

- *sukně* – skirt
- *jeans* or *džíny* – jeans, casual slacks
- *spodní prádlo* – underwear
- *ponožky* – socks
- *bunda* – outerwear jacket
- *bačkory* – slippers (An essential item in any Czech household, as shoes are never worn indoors.)

Shoes

These are an important item in a country which has a lot of cobble-stone streets and suffers long, cold, wet winters. You are probably best off bringing what shoes you need from home, as you can be assured of quality and expectations. That said, there are many places to buy and repair shoes in Prague. The local leader is Baťa, based in the central Moravian town of Zlín, who market their product all over the world; they are perhaps one of the largest and best known Czech corporations and do make a decent shoe.

Useful Words

- *obuv* or *boty* – shoes
- *prodejna bot, obuv* – shoe store
- *opravna bot* – shoe repair
- *krém na boty* – shoe polish
- *tkaničky* – shoe laces

HOUSEHOLD FURNISHINGS

This is something you need to decide before you come: do you want a furnished or an unfurnished home? If you want your own furniture, you'll have to arrange shipping, and then will not be too concerned with the information in this section. Department stores and furniture shops (*nábytek*) are reasonably well supplied, though you may have to make your selection and then order from the shop, which can take a few weeks. Prague has two IKEA outlets which are life-savers to many foreigners.

Useful Words

- *nábytek* – furniture
- *kancelářský nábytek* – office furniture
- *postel* – bed
- *deka, přikryvka* – blanket
- *lužkoviny* – sheets, linens
- *polstář* – pillow
- *stůl* – desk/table
- *lampa* – lamp
- *židle* – chair
- *křeslo* – armchair
- *šatna* – closet
- *skříň* – wardrobe
- *knihovna* – bookshelf

Electrical Appliances

Most apartments come with basic kitchen appliances, so you won't need to bring these with you. All brand-name electrical appliances, from radios to fax machines to dishwashers, are readily available at shops throughout the country.

See the note on electricity in the Housing section for information on different voltages in the Czech Republic.

Useful Terms

- *telefon* – telefon
- *televize* – television
- *satelit* – satellite
- *rádio* – radio
- *hi-fi* – stereo system
- *computer, počítač* – computer
- *lednička* or *lednice* – refrigerator
- *mrazák* – freezer
- *pračka* – washing machine

- *sušička* – dryer
- *myčka* – dishwasher
- *sporák* – stove
- *elektrický vařič* – hotplate
- *mikrovlná trouba* – microwave
- *žehlička* – iron

GIFTS

A major source of income from tourists, typical Czech household decorations also make the living experience here a bit more authentic. The most noted gifts and trinkets, which are not just touristy but a part of every Czechs' daily life, include Bohemian crystal, lace, wooden toys and puppets, and the ever-popular beer and Becherovka herb liquor. Touristy areas throughout the country are a surprisingly good place to buy these things: they have the best selection and prices are not too bad. These types of things make good gifts for yourself and your friends at home, but it would be the proverbial carrying coals to Newcastle to offer them to a Czech friend.

Available from the lace market, Czech lace is found in all homes and is a popular gift for tourists.

WEIGHTS AND MEASURES
- *deset deka* – 10 decigrams = 100 grams
- *dvacet deka* – 20 decigrams = 200 grams
- *třicet deka* – 30 decigrams = 300 grams
- *čtyřicet deka* – 40 decigrams = 400 grams
- *půl kila* – half-kilogram = roughly one pound

- 1 kilogram = approx. 2.2 pounds
- 1 pound = almost 0.5 kilograms
- 4 litres = roughly 1 gallon
- 1 litre = approx. 2 pints

TRANSPORTATION
Prague Mass Transit
Prague has an excellent, efficient public transport system, which most of the city relies on daily. In fact, the Prague metro claims to be the most heavily used underground system, per capita, in the world. It was inaugurated in 1974, and many of the older stations are hilarious testaments to Communist ideology, with plaques and statues dedicated to "the working people of Prague" and "the memory of the liberation of Prague by the Red Army in 1945." Trams and buses fill in where the metro doesn't go, and there is a comprehensive system of night transport between the hours of midnight and 4.30 am.

Tickets for individual journeys are very cheap, even if the system is confusing. A 10 Kč ticket allows you to make a single journey using any combination of transport, and a 6 Kč ticket is good for a journey of up to four stops on the metro or of 15 minutes above ground. Tickets can be purchased from the orange machines in every metro station, or from most newsagents around town. Tickets must then be stamped at the entrance gates to metro stations, and must similarly be validated in the little boxes you see hanging on poles in buses and trams. Note that tickets cannot be purchased on board a bus or tram, so it's a good idea to stock up.

Trams and buses complement the well used metro system. Prague has an excellent public transport network.

The reason you won't see too many other people validating tickets is that most Praguers possess a system pass, which allows unlimited use of the metro, buses, and trams for a remarkably low price. Passes can be purchased for a period of one, three, six, or twelve months, starting on the first day of that respective period – meaning passes are valid from the first to the last day of every calendar month, quarter, half-year, or year. Buy your base pass *(legitimace)* at a metro station ticket window (not all stations have such windows), and insert a passport photo. For each respective calendar term, you buy a small stamp (called a *kupon)* which you insert into the little plastic window.

Transport officials carry out random spot-checks, so while it may seem that you don't need to pay your way, you can hit an angry ticket-controller and face a fine for 'riding black.'

Metro trains run every 3–6 minutes during the day. Buses and trams are almost as frequent. Each bus and tram stop is marked by a signpost with the name of the stop and a schedule of times.

It is important to give up your seat to an elderly or disabled person on any public transport vehicle. You'll notice people offering their seats to the *babičky* (old ladies) who putter around the trams, and this is in fact part of the system's regulations.

Taxis

Prague's taxis carry a deservedly bad reputation. They are notorious rip-off artists, and for the most part are daring and obnoxious drivers. Taxis are not regulated by the city and can thus legally charge outlandish rates to gullible foreigners. Each taxi company (or independent operator) should have the rate posted on the door of the cab and should have a meter inside to measure this. Since deregulation came into effect in October 1996, the market has seemed to bear a rate of 16–20 Kč/kilometre. Check this before you get in and insist on a meter or agree to pay a price beforehand – and proceed with caution. There are a couple of reputable agencies in Prague which provide door-to-door service, and speak English: AAA Radiotaxi Nonstop (tel. 33 99 direct, or 312 2112), and Profi Taxi (tel. 6104 5555, 6104 5550).

Domestic Transportation

The country has a remarkably efficient and cheap bus and train network. Although the standard is nothing to shout about, both systems usually operate right on schedule.

The bus system is the most comprehensive, and many people use it in favour of the railways because it's often faster. There are direct buses between Prague and virtually all sizable towns throughout the country, whereas many rail journeys involve a change. Tickets are usually purchased on board from the driver, though on Friday afternoons and Sunday evenings, it's a good idea to try to get a seat reservation in advance, as the system is jammed with people going home or to the country for the weekend. To do this, you have to go to the station at which the bus originates. In Prague, tickets for all buses can be purchased from the main bus station at Florenc up to one week in advance. One distinct problem with the bus system is that the schedule is virtually impossible to decipher, and information windows are invariably rude and unhelpful. Having a Czech speaker on hand is immensely helpful.

Most cities are served by trains as well, though there is only a limited number of trunk lines radiating out from Prague, slowing down the proceedings considerably. The main rail lines from Prague head in the directions of Nürnberg (via Cheb and Plzeň), Berlin (via Dresden and Děčín), Ostrava (via Pardubice and Olomouc), Bratislava (via Brno), and České Budějovice. Train tickets can be bought at the station, and it is not necessary to do so in advance. Schedules are easy to figure out; just look for the yellow sign boards indicating departure (versus the white boards which are for arrivals).

Cars

Czechs for the most part are horrible drivers, plain and simple. It's not that they don't know how to drive, it's that they take the rules of the road much more liberally than they should. Speed limits are often ignored, lane changes can be sudden, and tailgating is common practice; hence, the accident rates are about double what they are in the US. I drive most days in Prague (not out of choice but on company business), and I don't exaggerate in saying that I see on average two accidents a week.

One thing that always strikes me when I return to the US is how slowly people drive, and how wide the streets are. Czechs always seem to be in a mad rush on the road – even Prague's narrow one-way streets can be made to feel like a racecourse, and if you're going slower than the guy on the highway behind you wants to, you'll be shot past and glared at as if you'd committed some rude act.

Driving in Prague is particularly nerve-wracking; it simply isn't made for cars. Many of its streets are one-way, many are torn up sporadically as pipe lines are replaced, and many are cobblestoned. When these are wet, drive especially carefully, as they can slip out from under you like ice. Many main streets have tram lines as well, some of which run down the middle or off to the side, though many share a single lane with cars.

Beware of the usual rush hours – approximately 6–9 am and 3–6 pm. Traffic patterns in Prague are a confounding mystery—some days it all moves smoothly enough, and some days it can be so bad you may as well just leave your vehicle where it is and take a tram.

Speed limits in towns and cities, including Prague, is 60 km/hour unless otherwise noted. On two-lane country roads it's 90 km/hour, and on highways (four-lane highways and roads marked in yellow on your road atlas) it's 110 km/hour, though most drivers tend to ignore all of these. There are far fewer traffic police on the road here than in some countries, so it's not such a risk to speed.

When a policeman does pull you over for a moving violation, he can fine you up to 1000 Kč. Note the 'up to' – it depends on how serious your offence is and what is the officer's mood at the time. For a minor violation you can probably talk him down to, say, 200 Kč (I've done this on a few occasions myself), though if you deserve it, he'll nail you, and you're expected to pay in cash on the spot. Ask to have him write up a proper ticket to insure that it doesn't go into his pocket – the temptation to do so must be irresistible.

Drinking and driving is a serious offence here, and police often do random spot-checks at night. Any hint of alcohol showing up in a breathalyser is enough to do you in (the legal limit is 0.08%), and penalties can range from a 10,000 Kč fine to confiscation of your license to imprisonment. Don't to it.

Car Ownership and Documentation

A regular driver's license issued from any European or North American country is valid here. An International Driver's License comes in handy if you hail from elsewhere.

If you own a car which was manufactured in Europe, your registration procedure is much smoother than if you ship it from overseas. I strongly recommend not doing the latter: it is costly and immensely frustrating and time-consuming. Speak with your dealer at home for information, and consider the following general procedures:

Non-Czechs must first have a valid long-stay permit ("green card") before they begin the registration procedure. First go to the traffic police *(dopravní inspektorát)* in your city (in Prague this is located at Kongresová 2, Prague 4, tel. 6118 1111, 6118 5383 – but don't expect them to speak English!), where you pick up a registration form *(přihlášení vozidla)*. Then you must proceed to an inspection station *(STK)* for a general inspection, and then to another facility where they inspect the catalytic converter. You must schedule these appointments yourself, and can obtain numbers at the traffic police office. Once you have all the necessary approvals, return to the traffic police where they issue your papers and license plates.

To use any of the country's four-lane highways, you must have a 400 Kč sticker visible in your windshield – this can be purchased from any border crossing or post office, and is valid for one calendar year.

Insurance is not required here, though judging from the number of wild drivers out there, you'd be irresponsible not to have it. If you're bringing your own car, contact one of the foreign insurance companies mentioned in the Insurance section below, or contact an office of Česká pojišt'ovna, the largest Czech insurance company. In Prague their central office is at Spálená 14, Prague 1, tel. 2409 2111, 2491 5594. In case of an accident, you must not move the vehicle from the spot at which it stopped moving. A police car will come around and monitor the situation.

If you run into trouble on the road (e.g. dead battery, flat tyre), call 6731 0713 for English-speaking assistance.

Roadsigns and Rules of the Road

Czech roadsigns are the same as those throughout Europe; if you've never driven in Europe be aware of a few differences:

A sign with a yellow diamond indicates that you are on the main road, with right-of-way over all incoming traffic. Many intersections don't have stop signs, as they use this right-of-way system instead. As you approach an intersection, watch for the yellow diamond; it will often be accompanied by a scheme of the upcoming intersection, with a thick line indicating the main road, and thinner lines coming into it. In similar fashion, if you approach an intersection and the scheme indicates you are not on the main road, you'll have to yield to incoming traffic. The reason for these signs is that it is not always clear who should have right-of-way.

A circular blue sign with a red X means no parking any time; with a red slash means no standing any time, and hence, no parking.

Trams always have priority – if you're blocking a tram track, and the streetcar driver in either direction wants to go ahead, he can smash you and it will be your fault. Be careful when making a turn.

Parking in Prague

Not only was this city not made for driving, it was certainly not made for parking either. City planners, from the Přemysls to the Communists, were woefully blind to future trends in this regard, and the ever-increasing number of cars on the road has made parking a real problem. All sorts of illegal parking jobs are performed daily, whether it's simply ignoring the 'No Parking' signs, parking in someone else's reserved spot, double parking, parking in front of a garage entrance, or driving up onto the sidewalk. I confess I've done all of the above at one time or another.

The traffic police do monitor the situation, and are now quick to place boots (clamps) on errantly-parked vehicles. If this happens to you, they will leave a sticker on the driver's side window, with a number to call; tell them the street name and nearest building address and they should come within 20 minutes to relieve you. The fine for this indiscretion is 500 Kč.

The chaotic compactness of the centre should be enough to convince you to leave your vehicle at home and take the metro. For those who must drive, though, there are zoning regulations for the city centre. Certain streets are reserved for short-term parking (up to 2 hours), others for mid-term (up to 6 hours), and others for those who have Prague 1 parking permits. Short-term parking is monitored either by an attendant or by a meter, for which you pay 20–30 Kč per hour.

Parking permits for Prague 1 (city centre) are issued to residents of that district and to companies who pay for the privilege. It is possible to reserve a spot on the street anywhere in the city, which will be marked by a sign with either your company name or your car's license number. This is a pretty good way to insure yourself a parking spot, though it would still take a while to call a tow-truck if someone decides to ignore the sign. Such reserved spots cost a whopping 45,000 Kč per year.

Reserved street parking does not protect you against car theft or break-in, which is a serious problem in Prague. Protect your car with an alarm, a steering-wheel clamp, and whatever other measures you can.

Třeboň, in south Bohemia – a typical town square with Gothic and Baroque features. It may take a while to become accustomed to the system of street names and building addresses but the architecture offers a pleasant distraction.

Streets Names and Building Addresses

Streets almost never have the word 'street' or 'avenue' written; instead it's just the name and number. Building numbers always follow the street name.

You may be confused to see two addresses written on an envelope or letterhead, and two signs with different numbers on the building itself; for example, you may see the address Purkyňova 53/4, and when you go to the building you'll see a blue sign with the 4 and a red sign with the 53. The number on the red sign, usually the longer number, is the building plot number, which used to be used as the address until someone figured out that these numbers don't necessarily go in order. So a new logical numbering system was developed, and blue signs were placed on buildings in the order they stand on the street. These are generally the ones used now – why they keep the old numbers is a mystery.

RECYCLING

There are facilities throughout the country for recycling of glass and paper products. Keep an eye out for large coloured bins on street corners, with signs indicating their intended contents. Recycling of aluminium cans is not in practice here, mainly because most drinks are sold in glass bottles.

Drinks that are sold in glass bottles, such as beer, wine, and some soft drinks, have a 3 Kč per bottle deposit tacked on. Bottles can then be returned to the place of purchase, or to any shop that sells similar shaped bottles, for a cash return.

MEDIA
The Printed Press

Competition in the newspaper and magazine field in Prague is ferocious. This city of 1.3 million people supports some 15 daily papers of all editorial slants. Some are of excellent quality and some are trash, and the locals eat them up, often buying two or three to get them through the day. This isn't hard to do – all newspapers are compact, concise publications of about 25 pages, with condensed news stories and not much advertising, making it a quick task to read. Of course, it will take quite a while to develop your Czech language skills to a level of comprehension. Attempting to read the daily paper is a great way to build vocabulary though.

The best, straightforward, unbiased papers are probably *Mladá Fronta Dnes* and *Lidové Noviny*. Right-leaning papers include *Denní Telegraf* and *Český Týdeník*, while leftist publications include the still popular former Communist party rag *Právo* (formerly *Rudé Právo*). Specialised papers include *Hospodářské noviny*, a business daily, *Práce*, the Czech Trade Union daily, and *Sport*. Sliding rapidly down the quality scale are the sensationalist papers *Blesk, Expres,* and *Večerník Praha.*

English Language News

The established source of English-language news in Prague is *The Prague Post*. It appears every Wednesday and is available from many newsagents throughout Prague and larger cities in the country. The emphasis is on local news, with sections on business and finance, sports, culture, travel, and an extensive rundown of the week's entertainment. At 40 Kč per issue, it's not particularly cheap, though it's invaluable if you want to know what's going on.

Other, more business oriented papers include the *Central European Business Weekly*, and the new *Prague Business Journal*. *The Prague Tribune* is a news/business/culture magazine published in English and French. *Pozor* is the latest in a long line of culture-oriented news magazines.

Major international papers can be bought from newsagents in central Prague, though are hard to come by elsewhere. These include the current day's issues of *The International Herald Tribune, USA Today International, The Guardian, Frankfurter Allgemeine, Le Monde*, and other major Western publications. Magazines such as *Time, Newsweek, Figaro, L'Express, Stern,* even *National Geographic, Rolling Stone,* and *Elle* (in Czech!) are often available as well.

TV and Radio Broadcasting

There are four regular network TV channels in the Czech Republic: ČT 1 and 2, TV Nova, and Prima. Česká Televise, the state TV service, operates ČT 1 and 2, similar in content to the BBC networks in Great Britain. TV Nova is a new American joint-venture which has swept the market since its inception in early 1994. Prima is an Italian joint-venture, in operation since 1992. All four networks have Czech and foreign programs and films, usually dubbed into Czech. American and British soap operas and comedies are very popular. Specific program information can be found in most newspapers as well as the *Pro-Gram* magazine guide, available at most newsstands.

News in English airs on ČT 2 weekdays 8–8.45 am, and weekends 7–8 am, though these times tend to shift around at random.

Satellite and cable TV are becoming popular; both are dominated by German channels, though CNN, Eurosport, MTV, and other English-language stand-bys are available depending on what programming your dish receives. Not all homes have cable or satellite hook-ups.

Radio broadcasting is excellent. For news in English, the BBC comes in on FM radio 101.1, with news at the top of the hour round the clock. Broadcasts in French and German are also receivable. Prague has several rock/pop stations (88.2 FM, 91.9 FM, 93.7 FM, 98.1 FM, and 99.7 FM to name a few) as well as classical (98.7 FM), jazz (97.2 FM), and Europe's only exclusively country radio station (89.5 FM).

There is a monthly service charge of 50 Kč for TV and 20 Kč for radio; the bill comes in the mail and is payable at any post office.

POSTAL SERVICES

Post offices in the Czech Republic serve not only the purpose of sending mail, but also of paying many bills. There are different windows for buying stamps, paying your utility bills, and if you live in a state apartment, paying rent. Post offices are open Monday to Friday 8 am–6 pm, except for the Main Post Office in Prague, at Jindřříšská 14 just off Wenceslas Square, which is open 24 hours.

Mail service costs are remarkably cheap; in fact the rates actually went down in January 1996, yet speed of delivery is at least as good as anywhere else. A regular letter sent to or received from North America takes about seven days. Within Europe it takes about five days, and within the country it should be a two day job, though as anywhere, you shouldn't necessarily count on these times. All mail is priced according to weight, so unless you are only sending one page letters or post cards, you'll probably want to visit the post office directly to have your mail properly stamped. Mail sent within Europe is automatically sent air mail, though if you are sending mail overseas, be sure to write *par avion* or *letecký*, or ask for an air mail sticker from the post office.

If speed is of the essence, you can send letters *expres*, and if you need security you can send them *doporučený* (registered), both of which cost about double the normal rate. To send a registered letter, look for the small slips of paper marked *podácí lístek*, which usually sit in a pile on the counter. Fill in the sender's address on the top line, and your address on the line below it.

Parcels over two kilograms must pass customs clearance, which is quite a confusing process if you don't speak Czech. The main post office of most cities has a customs department, which will provide you with forms to fill out. They may inspect the contents of your package as well. In Prague, there is a special customs post office, which you must visit if you are sending or receiving heavy packages. It is located at Plzeňská 129, Prague 5. Bring a Czech speaker along with you to avoid immense frustration.

All post offices have a *poste restante* (general delivery) service. In Prague, this is commonly done at the Main Post Office; if you want letters sent to one closer to you, find out the address of that post office. Be sure to have *poste restante* written under your name.

Utility bills are paid at the post office as well – though you may have an arrangement with your landlord that he pays the bills for you. If you pay bills yourself, take them to the window marked *výplata/ příjem peněz*, hand the bills and the cash (no other method of payment is accepted) to the teller, and take your receipt. Not a word of spoken Czech is required other than "thank you."

Courier Services

All the big international courier services, such as FedEx, DHL, UPS, and so on, have offices in Prague. Note that the cost of sending letters or packages through them is significantly more expensive than in many other countries.

TELEPHONES

A well worn joke here is that half the country is waiting for a telephone, and the other half is waiting for the dial tone. The telephone system runs on the same principle as the housing market – not enough supply for the demand, but it is improving.

You cannot simply request a telephone and expect to get it. Thousands of Czech families have lived for years without a phone, as the previous regime found it undesirable to install enough phone lines for the submissive masses. Be sure that your flat does have a telephone that is already installed. It is not uncommon for a landlord to say, "it will be installed soon," which translates to waiting for Godot.

Telephone service is fast improving with the help of various foreign telecommunications firms, but the quality, again, can be dubious. You may have to dial two or three times before you get through, and you may be able to overhear other people's conversations as the lines sometimes get crossed. Telephones occasionally stop working for no apparent reason, then come back on a few days later. It's frustrating, but there's little that can be done. Radio phones can now be ordered and installed through the phone company in parts of the country in a few weeks. Mobile phones are now huge business and the network is developing with the market.

Not all apartments have phones with independent lines – some are shared lines and some are the old-fashioned party line – a trunk line comes into the building and then divides into different numbers for the occupants of the building. So it's quite possible that you won't be able to use your phone because someone else in the building is on it. Verify the situation before you sign your name on the lease.

Your phone bill is supposed to come monthly, though this is not always the case. When it does come, you pay the bill at the post office.

Note that telephone numbers have anywhere from 4 to 8 digits, and there is no real rhyme or reason to it, except that 8-digit numbers are generally used by offices in the central districts of major cities.

It is important to have a telephone card if you ever need to use public phones, as there are very few coin phones around. Phonecards can be purchased at newsagents *(tabák or trafika)* and at post offices, and work on a principle of subtracting units from the amount on it. This figure will appear on a little window on the telephone. A phone call within the area code will deduct one unit (2 Kč) every three minutes during peak times (7:00 am–4:00 pm) and every six minutes at other times. A long-distance call within the country will deduct a unit every minute; and if you're calling out of the country, you'll watch the numbers shoot down as you speak.

MOVING COMPANIES

If you're shipping large amounts of furniture and other personal belongings, contact an international moving company or relocation service in your home town; these are always listed in the phone book. Companies such as Allied Pickfords and AGS have offices in Prague.

PUBLIC TOILETS

There's not too much to be said here, except that toilets in public areas such as train stations and cheap pubs can be pretty foul. Not only are they dirty and smelly, you often have to pay for them! There's usually a poor old pensioner sitting inside who collects your 2 Kč and hands you a puny piece of non-absorbent toilet paper if you need it. There are very few public toilets on the street. Prague's metro system has rest rooms in each station, and some cities have public facilities in parks, though many men have no qualms about finding the nearest tree.

LAUNDRY SERVICES

There aren't too many of these around. Most Czechs have their own washing machine at home, so there isn't much need for public laundromats.

Old-fashioned laundry maid services are available from a few *prádelna* shops that you find around town. These are mostly used by hotels and restaurants, though it is possible to give them your load of laundry and have them do it for you.

Prague now has a few Western-style laundromats where you can do the wash yourself, though it's not cheap. The following have good quality washing machines and dryers, for around 50 Kč per machine per load:

• Prague Laundromat, Korunní 14, Prague 2, metro náměstí Míru
• Laundry Kings, Dejvická 16, Prague 6, metro Hradčanská

Chapter Eight

SETTLING IN

HOUSING

Finding housing in Prague is a real game involving lots of searching, negotiating, and compromising. In the rest of the country, the real estate market is not as well established and you may have to rely on contacts from work to help secure a place. Either way, you can expect to take lots of time and either spend lots of money or make lots of concessions. If you have a high standard, you'll likely find close to what you want eventually, but you'll pay through the nose and may have to make a sacrifice or two anyway. If you're on a low budget, it's a matter of luck and quite probably lowering your standard. Don't get discouraged; you'll find something eventually. And remember that the extra money you spend on housing can be made up on the cheaper costs of things such as food, entertainment, and travel.

Many people come to Prague expecting to live in beautiful apartments in the Old Town, yet soon find out that such properties command top dollar. Real estate prices in the capital are on par with Paris, Tokyo or New York, whether this reflects quality or not. Again, flexibility is your greatest asset.

This is the Situation

An explanation of the housing situation is necessary here to understand what is a particularly complicated issue. Until the real estate market unravels itself from the former regime (which will take many years) a two-tiered system is in effect: Czech natives living in state-owned properties still pay fixed rents of as low as US$50 per month, while foreigners are usually forced to pay hundreds or thousands of dollars for their apartment or villa of choice. Landlords often try to get foreign tenants, who can usually pay much more than Czechs.

Under Communism, people were simply assigned housing by the authorities, with respect to family size but not to location. One could not simply decide to move or to rent one's apartment out without proper authority. Housing was controlled to such an extent that everything was kept to a bare minimum: waiting lists several thousand names long still sit on housing authorities' desks somewhere, and many people are forced to share apartments with family members and acquaintances in the meantime. In some cases students and young adults still live with their parents, and separated couples even continue to share flats! Now that real estate is integrating into the market economy, locals seeking housing are subject to the same rent costs as foreigners, though they often don't have the same resources.

The massive grey housing projects you see on the outskirts of all Czech cities were built as a quick-fix solution to housing: these *panelák* (prefab) apartment buildings are functional to an extreme: not only are they aesthetically revolting, the apartments therein are tiny and uniformly cheap. Yet families live in them just as anywhere – whether you were assigned a flat in a *panelák* or in a classy neighbourhood was a matter of pure chance. Because of this, the *sidlíště* ('housing estates,' as they euphemistically call them) are nothing like the housing projects of an American inner-city. In fact, there are some advantages to them: heat and hot water always work well, bus or tram service to the centre (or the nearest metro) is always excellent, and there are shopping centres and schools in the immediate vicinity.

At the same time, many older apartment buildings have deteriorated to abominable conditions. Utilities occasionally fail, public hallways haven't been painted in years, and there is precious little money for surface or structural improvements. Those fortunate enough to own their property, or those who have permission granted from the city to sublet them, are in a privileged position indeed – if they can do a good reconstruction job, their property becomes part of an exclusive pool of attractive homes. Many relocating foreigners simply cannot bear the lower standard of housing in general, and are thus forced to pay large sums for good standard.

Who Owns Your Apartment

There are three types of landlords, or lessors: (1) the city or state; (2) a cooperative, meaning a Czech legal entity which has purchased and invested in a building, and whose members include the building's tenants; and (3) a person or company who has either bought a property or regained it through restitution, and is thus the private owner.

If a building is owned by the city or state, and many still are, the tenant who has legal rights to a flat may rent it with permission from the city or state. The tenant is thus the lessee, and the person to whom he rents it is the subtenant. If you rent a city or state owned apartment from a lessee who has not been granted permission to do so, the lease is illegal and both you and your 'landlord' can be evicted from the premises. The likelihood of anyone catching up to you is very low indeed (I admit to having 'squatted' in this way for two years), but exercise caution.

If a cooperative owns the building, the tenants within have a sort of membership status and can basically do what they want with their flat; they do officially need to be granted permission to sublet from the cooperative as a whole, but this is merely a formality. The city or state plays no role in this procedure.

If a private individual or a company owns the building, he is the official landlord, and a lease agreement is negotiated directly with him.

How to Find Housing

You have three options in finding a place to live:

- Check with friends and colleagues. If you are replacing somebody at work, you may want to consider renting his or her apartment, or if you have contacts in the city, scour around and see what they may come up with. If you're on a low budget, this is a good way to finagle something.

- Check the classifieds newspaper *Annonce* (it appears in two editions – ask for section A), sold every Monday, Wednesday, and Friday at any newsagent. There are lengthy listings of apartments and houses for rent, which you'll need Czech-speaking skills to decipher. Thousands of people rely on *Annonce*, so start first thing in the morning, work the phones immediately, and get out to see places as soon as possible.

- Use a real estate agent. For many, this is the only way. Because many landlords want to rent their apartments and villas to foreigners (at Western rent levels or higher) they go directly to agents who specialise in such dealings. Many real estate offices in Prague in fact deal exclusively with a foreign clientele, and a network has developed amongst agencies, Western companies, and landlords. Be careful, though, whom you choose. It's no problem to use more than one agency, but be sure to contact one that advertises itself in both English and Czech, and that has experienced agents on staff. Likewise, there is no listings system, so real estate companies often share properties. All agencies charge commissions to the tenant, usually of one month's rent; most agencies usually take a month from the landlord as well.

  A distinct advantage to working with a good agency is that they do all the work for you, which includes finding property and scheduling visits, translating an agreement with the landlord, and signing a legally binding contract. Be sure in choosing an agency that they use a lawyer who is experienced with this complex procedure. I can personally recommend Prague Realty Services,

Korunní 127, Praha 3, tel. 6731 1216, fax. 744 053.

Once the deal is inked, you should be set. Czech landlords seem to have finally learned that once they rent their apartment under contract, they cannot do things like enter at their own free will, or raise the rent without warning. This was a problem in the early 1990s.

Price

Now the fun begins. The chances of actually finding a home suited to your needs for a standard Czech price are slim to none, so be prepared to spend at least what you are accustomed to spending at home, and quite likely more. The market is still volatile, although price patterns have developed. Rent prices are often quoted in Deutsche Marks (DM), due to the perceived greater stability of that currency. Payments are usually accepted in Czech crowns (Kč), however.

For a quality two or three-room flat in or around the centre, you can expect to pay at least 1500 DM per month, though more likely up to 3000 DM. Larger, luxurious flats in the centre can go for 3500 DM or more. Further away from centre, though still within easy commuting distance, prices lower a bit — from approximately 1200 DM and up for a small flat to 2000–3000 DM for a larger flat. A small, modest house will cost from 2000–2500 DM, and luxury villas, especially those in Prague 6, go for 4000 DM and up.

If you're really scraping the barrel you may have to settle for a place in the *paneshlák*s, which can be had for around 400–600 DM, or you may get lucky with a place in a working-class neighbourhood such as Žižkov or Smíchov for the same price.

What to Consider

An interesting phenomenon seems to take place among expatriates relocating in Prague. Those who are accustomed to driving up to an hour to work every day and sending the kids to faraway schools refuse to live the same way in Prague; because the city is so compact, they

147

insist on having a place in or near the centre, or near the international schools, most of which are in Prague 6. Don't be too sold on living in Pragues 1 or 6 – these are generally perceived as the glamour districts, though in fact there are plenty of other nice areas, often in cheaper rent categories.

The guide to Prague's districts below should help in deciding where to live. Remember that Prague has an excellent public transit system, so even if you live in an area that feels far away, it's probably not more than 20–30 minutes to the centre.

PRAGUE BY DISTRICT

Prague is divided into ten districts, each of which is loosely subdivided into neighbourhoods. The following is a summary of each district, with positive and negative points on each.

Prague 1 is the central area, which includes the Old Town, Malá Strana (the Little Quarter or Lesser Town) and the castle district. The advantages to living in Prague 1 are obvious – it is beautiful, historical, and dead central, but there are certain disadvantages too. Because the city lies in a valley, the air in Prague 1 is about the worst. Parking is very difficult to find, and certain streets can be noisy, particularly at night.

Prague 2 includes the close-in residential neighbourhoods of Vinohrady and the New Town (Nové Město) along the river. Because of its pleasant surroundings, easy access to shopping and nightlife, and well connected transportation lines, Prague 2 is in high demand.

Prague 3 is an interesting blend of pleasant neighbourhoods and working-class grit, located just off-centre and to the east. Prague 3 borders on Vinohrady to the south, thus including many of Vinohrady's architectural and residential advantages, though it is largely made up of the historically working-class area known as Žižkov. All of Prague 3 is well served by public transportation, shopping, and nightlife.

Prague 4 is difficult to characterise, as it is spreads over the entire southern sector of the city east of the river. Closer-in areas, bordering

A view of Prague, from above the Vltava River.

Prague 2, have some fine apartment buildings and views; further-out areas contain fine villas at rents lower than in Prague 6 – in fact many people overlook Prague 4 in the rush for Prague 6, which is a mistake. Prague 4's disadvantages are mainly that it contains vast tracts of *panelák* buildings, a huge eyesore. Direct transportation links can be scarce; many trips involve a bus ride to the metro or tram.

Prague 5 covers the southwestern suburbs across the river from Prague 4, and contains everything from the dirty section of Smíchov along the river to impressive villas (with great views) high up on the hills of Barrandov to the enormous grey *paneláks* of Jihozápadné město. Prague 5 has some fine parks and relatively clean air. Transportation is good, though you may need to catch a bus to the metro.

Prague 6 is generally regarded as the city's most prestigious district after Prague 1. The Dejvice and Hanspaulka areas in particular are home to many foreign businesspeople (not to mention President Havel and Prime Minister Klaus). The area has many embassies and

149

fine villas, and is close to the airport and nice parks. Families often choose to live here for the proximity to most of the international schools, though prices here are amongst the highest in the city. Most public transportation connections to the centre involve a tram or bus to the metro.

Prague 7 includes the commercial/residential Holešovice and Letná areas tucked in the loop of the river Vltava, plus a piece of land called Troja just north of the river. The fantastic parks Letná and Stromovka take up sizable chunks of the area, and much of Troja is occupied by the Prague zoo. The inner loop of the river has excellent metro and tram service.

Prague 8 occupies the northern section of town, and except for the metro which runs through the rundown Libeň neighbourhood, most of the district feels far out and decrepit. The Kobylisy neighbourhood does have a few nice homes, however.

Prague 9 disappears off the map to the northeast and is too far away and too unattractive for most. If you happen to work in the area, though, you can probably find a good home for significantly cheaper rent than anywhere else in town.

Prague 10 wedges itself in alongside Pragues 2 and 3, then spreads out into east-southeastern infinity. Close-in Prague 10 offers some fine residential neighbourhoods – Vršovice and parts of Strašnice, for example, are no different from Vinohrady in appearance and are similarly well-connected, and nice apartment buildings, detached homes, and row houses exist elsewhere. Much of the district, however, is similar to Prague 9 – far away and industrial.

GENERAL STANDARDS

Standards of quality of flats and houses vary widely, and it is important to be certain of what you want and what you can expect.

Older flats are often spacious, while newer ones can be pretty cramped. Size of flats is always referred to in square metres and in number of rooms (not number of bedrooms), plus a kitchen. Therefore a 3+1 flat has three rooms and a separate kitchen. Because of housing assignments, Czechs often live in flats that serve the bare minimum of necessity. A family of four may occupy a small apartment with two bedrooms, a living room, kitchen, and one bathroom.

Kitchens normally contain a sink and countertop, cabinet space, stove/oven, and refrigerator/freezer, the appliances usually being on the small side. Dishwashers are rare. Washing machines are quite common, though are small, and are usually located in the bathroom; dryers are rare, and Czechs usually hang laundry up to dry above the bathtub or on the balcony.

Bathrooms normally have a tub, though sometimes only a shower. Tubs for some reason almost never have shower curtains or shower hooks, though there is always a detachable hose. The hot water boiler often hangs above the tub, and if it's an older model you'll be able to see the flames from the gas boiler. Toilets (WC) are usually in a cubicle separate from the bathroom.

Flats are often rented unfurnished, though some, especially in the lower price range, come furnished. Furnished flats and houses should include the following: bed(s), table(s), desk(s), chairs, wardrobe or closet space, chest of drawers, wall units or bookshelves, curtains, and basic kitchen appliances. Check about silverware, and pots and pans, and linens; furnished flats may or may not include these.

If you take a furnished place, you will not need to buy much, if anything else, though old Czech furniture can indeed be quite old. Single beds are generally narrow, while double beds are often in the form of a unit with two single mattresses laid together, not a queen or king-size mattress. Sheets and blankets are not normally used, rather a thick duvet wrapped in a sheet is used to cover the bed year round. Pillows are usually very large and fluffy. Most apartments have double windows, to help keep out the noise.

Buildings are often old and decrepit, with creaky lifts and peeling walls. Some are in decent condition, and a few have been nicely fixed up. All apartment buildings have a series of bells with names on the door outside so you can ring up. It is extremely rare to have a building porter or attendant, and tenants usually take turns sweeping or mopping the public areas. Most buildings are kept locked at all times, and every tenant has a key to the front door. Many apartment buildings have shops on the ground floor.

Because of chronic pollution, you may wish to invest in an air purifier. Also, because it is dry in the winter, a humidifier could come in handy.

Lifts

Many apartment buildings have lifts, but some do not. Nearly all lifts are slow and creaky, making you feel a bit nervous the first time you ride in them. Lifts operate on a system whereby you push a button to call the lift – but if the red light next to the button is on, the lift is already moving because someone else has called it or is in it. Lifts don't have any sort of memory here, so you have to wait until the light goes off, then push the button – you might want to stand with your finger poised over the button until the light goes off, to make sure you get to call it ahead of someone else on another floor. Similarly, if people going to different floors get in the lift at the same time, it is important to push the lowest floor number destination first, then when that person gets out, to push the next highest floor. You can avoid disgruntled neighbours by announcing your floor as you get in the lift. Most lifts have doors which must be closed before the lift can move. This is important to note especially when you get out – if you just walk off without closing the door properly, the elevator will just sit there, unusable to those on other floors. I have been forced to walk up five floors to my office on many occasions when someone who wasn't aware of this failed to close the door properly.

Student Accommodation
If you are a student, you will likely be assigned a room in a dormitory *(kolej)* which may be single or shared with a roommate or two. As universities don't have campuses as elsewhere, university dorms are scattered throughout the city. You'll likely have to use public transportation to get to classes every day. Dorm rooms have a bed, desk, lamp, linens, bookshelves, wardrobe, bathroom and toilet (often shared with suite-mates though sometimes in the corridor), and there is a community kitchen on each floor.

LEGALITIES AND TENANT RIGHTS
The same basic tenant rights apply here as elsewhere, assuming you have a legal lease. Lease contracts are usually signed for a period of one, two, or three years, often with an option-to-renew clause attached. There are no legal regulations regarding length periods – it's whatever you agree with the landlord. There is an official notice period of three months for both sides if either decides to break the lease with sufficient reason but actually tenants can leave without giving a reason after three months notice. Landlords are bound by a series of regulations outlined in the Czech Civil Code. Try to avoid inflation clauses – landlords sometimes try to write these into the contract after the second year or so.

153

Deposits are rarely demanded, though landlords often request advance payments of two months, sometimes more. Again, there are no regulations to this. If your landlord requests two months upon signing of the lease, you are not expected to pay rent again until the beginning of the third month. Many landlords do request telephone deposits, which are often calculated as the average monthly phone bill, paid two months prior to the end of the lease. Insurance on the premises is the responsibility of the landlord. If you bring or buy your own furniture, you must pay your own insurance for it.

Useful Words

- *byt* – flat or apartment
- *vila* or *rodinný dům* – detached or semidetached house. The word *vila* is used to avoid confusion over the word 'house,' *(dům* in Czech) which actually means 'building.'
- *zařizený* – furnished
- *nezařizený* – unfurnished
- *pronajmout* – to rent
- *k pronajmu* – for rent
- *pokoj* or *místnost* – room
- *kuchyň* – kitchen
- *koupelna* – bathroom
- *záchod* – toilet
- *sporák*—stove
- *telefon* – telephone
- *topení* – heat
- *elektrika* – electricity
- *plyn* – gas
- *voda* – water
- *přízemí* – ground floor
- *1. patro* – first floor
- *výtah* – lift (elevator)

UTILITIES

Utilities include gas/oil, water, electricity, sewage and waste removal, and building charges. Utilities for a family of four in a large apartment or house should cost 1000–2000 Kč per month altogether, depending of course on use. Note that landlords will want to keep the telephone bill separate, even if all other utilities are included in the lease, because of long-distance calls that foreigners are wont to make. Some landlords include utility bills up to a reasonable level, though utilities are usually paid in addition to the rent. This must be worked out on an individual basis. If you are paying your own utilities, you will receive the bills in the mail and will be expected to pay them in cash at the post office.

Electricity

The Czech Republic uses 220 AV and 60 cycles, in line with most of the rest of Europe. Plugs are of the large, round three-prong type. If you are coming from North America, which runs on 110 AV and 50 cycles, you will not be able to use your electrical appliances without an adaptor and transformer. These are easily obtainable at any electronics shop at home, though are difficult to find here, so be sure to stock up. Most appliances such as hairdryers, electric razors, and irons are best bought here, but if you're bringing anything that plugs into a wall, be sure to get the proper converters before you come.

SUPPORT GROUPS AND HOME HELP

You will likely find the expatriate community to be an invaluable source of support, both materially and emotionally. It's easy to get together with someone from your own country – colleagues from work or contacts from your children's school – and talk (or complain!) about the differences you are experiencing. This can be a great way to adjust to living in a foreign country, especially in the beginning, and it's easy to make new friends in this way. Try not to limit yourself, though; so many people come here and associate only with their own kind, and they really miss out on the most important part of living abroad, that is, assimilating into the local culture.

If you work, you are bound to come into contact with other expatriates, be it colleagues in your own company or business contacts that you're bound to make. Spouses often have difficulty, however, as they don't necessarily have the same network at hand. Many relocating families with children that I spoke with said that schools were the best source of support – there are lots of other parents in the same position, and all the international schools have regular functions such as picnics and ski trips to bring their communities together. Organisations such as parent-teacher associations and after-school programs also provide spouses the opportunity to do community and charity work. It's easy to mope when you've got little to do, and finding ways to keep yourself busy is the tried-and-true best method of avoiding lethargy and depression.

Prague has plenty of other organisations that serve as social focal points for foreigners. There are several groups, such as the International Church of Prague, the Open Prague Jewish Community, the International Women's Club of Prague, and various university clubs, which meet regularly for official, as well as social purposes. Such organisations advertise regularly in *The Prague Post*.

These are also a good source of information for help around the home. As services such as babysitting, cleaning, and catering are hard to come by here, use this built-in network to your advantage. One organisation in Prague, Affordable Luxuries, specialises in locating and providing such services: Affordable Luxuries, Štěpánská 15, Praha 2, tel. 216 1266, fax. 298 024.

INFORMATION SOURCES

The Prague Post is a good source of information on just about anything you need. Aside from news, they print a complete entertainment listing every week, and have a good classifieds section as well.

The Yellow Pages *(Zlaté stránky)* are provided for all homes and offices, with listings in Czech. If you don't know the Czech word for the category of goods or services you need, turn to the back, where they provide cross references in English and German.

For virtually all the information you need on everything from Czech parliament members to a list of foreign companies in the Czech Republic to lawyers and accountants to fine dining, get hold of the *Resources* guide. This is a black book of names and numbers, updated quarterly; all internationals doing business in Prague rely on it for well-organised, easy-to-find information. Contact them at Tĭpánská 15, 120 00 Praha 2, tel. 299 205, fax. 298 024.

LEGAL DOCUMENTS FOR LIVING AND WORKING

Work and residence permits need not be obtained before you arrive in the Czech Republic. They can be obtained here as long as you begin the process before your tourist visa or stamp expires, but beware, the process is long and complicated. Regulations change constantly, so the information provided here is a general guideline. It is important to employ the services of a good lawyer to help guide you through the maze of paperwork; if you are a student, your study-abroad program or the office of international students at your university should help.

If you intend to stay longer than the allowance on your passport stamp or tourist visa, you officially need a long-term stay permit. Many expats, however, get frustrated by the formalities and skip it; this is feasible (for example, you can go to Germany for the weekend and return with a new tourist entry stamp) though the government is now cracking down on such abusers. If you are legally employed or are related to someone who is legally employed, or are a student in the Czech Republic, and you have a legal residence, you can obtain a long-stay permit which entitles you to all advantages that Czechs have here – including state health insurance and local (rather than inflated tourist) prices in hotels.

There are plenty of excellent law firms in the country, including several international firms, which can be found in the Yellow Pages. Any of the major international consulting firms can help as well. One local lawyer in Prague that I can personally recommend is Mikuláš Ürge, Jungmannovo náměstí 3, 110 00 Praha 1, tel. 9000 1961-3; fax 2422 0113.

There are two types of long-stay permits beyond the regular tourist visa or passport stamp: (1) regular long-stay permit *(Průkaz o povolení k pobytu cizince)*, on which is noted your work and residence status, valid for up to one year with unlimited renewals; and (2) permanent residence permit – only available for reasons of marriage or other permanent relationship to Czech nationals.

In order to obtain a long-stay permit, you must have the following three documents:

- Proof of a clear criminal record in the Czech Republic and abroad.
- Residence permit
- Indication of a reason to stay (i.e. work permit, Czech trade licence, student visa, or relationship to someone with one of the above).

For all of these applications you will need to provide your passport; you should also be sure to bring all relevant marriage certificates, university diplomas, and trade licenses that you possess.

Verifying a Clear Criminal Record

This is a formality which must be done to assure the authorities that you have no outstanding record of criminal behaviour in the Czech Republic. Further inspection may also delve into the interpol network to verify that you are not a fugitive from elsewhere. To obtain your clear criminal record document, go to the general prosecution office, criminal record department (Rejstřík Trestu České republiky), náměstí Hrdinů 1300, 14066 Praha 4. (Other cities have their own offices.) Fill out a form, provide your passport, a copy of your birth certificate, and pay 60 Kč.

Obtaining a Residency Permit

To gain legal accommodation you must present an official sworn affidavit (*čestné prohlášení*), provided by the foreign police, which must be signed in front of a notary, and stating that your landlord is renting a living space to you and has the legal right to do so. All family members over the age of 6 need their own affidavit, so be sure that your landlord signs as many documents as there are family members.

Obtaining a Reason to Stay

There are officially five reasons to stay long-term in the Czech Republic.

- Ownership or co-ownership of a company legally established in the Czech Republic. Such a person does not need a work permit, rather he must provide: (a) the articles of association of the established company; (b) a trade license; and (c) proof that the company is registered in court.
- Sole entrepreneurship, that is, independent work in a practising trade, not necessarily in connection with any company; i.e., freelance work. Sole entrepreneurs come in various trades, which can be broken down into two main groups: (a) Those in regulated fields, such as law, medicine, dentistry, pharmaceuticals, restaurant and catering services, etc. Such persons who are professionally licensed in regulated trades in their home country need to obtain an equivalent qualification in the Czech Republic. (b) Those in special fields which do not have an accepted governing body, such as computer programmers, masseurs, brokers, advisors, freelance writers, etc. Sole entrepreneurs in non-regulated fields must obtain a trade licence (*živnostenský list*), of which there are many kinds.
- Employee status in a Czech legal entity, whether it is a Czech company or a foreign company legally established in the Czech Republic. This person then needs a work permit as his reason to stay. In order to protect Czech workers, the government has a

159

system whereby an employer who wants to hire a foreign worker must first be presented with potential Czech substitutes. The employer must register at the employment office in his Prague district, indicating that he has a vacancy; the employment office then has 21 days to send potential employees to the employer. The employer can refuse the offerings with a simple reason, then after 21 days proceed to the work permits office.

- Student enrolled in a school or university in the Czech Republic. Students can and should obtain a student visa before arrival in the Czech Republic, and then upon arrival obtain a long-stay permit. Your institution here will help.
- Permanent relationship to a long-term resident; i.e., a non-working spouse, or child over the age of six, of a foreigner working legally in the Czech Republic. Documents of relationship, such as marriage or birth certificates, are required.

Once all three relevant documents are obtained, proceed to the Foreign Police (*Cizinecká policie*) where you fill in an application, provide them with three passport photos and a stamp *(kolek)* for 1000 Kč (which can be purchased there), stand in line for several hours, then wait two to three months for them to issue your long-stay permit, affectionately known as a green card. (In Prague the address is Olšanská 3, Praha 3; other cities have their own offices.)

LEGALITIES FOR SETTING UP A COMPANY

There are four types of companies:

- s.r.o – *společnost s ručením omezeným* – limited liability company, in which the partners are limited to the registered capital investment.
- a.s. – *akciovná společnost* – a joint-stock company in which the holders of shares in the company have liability limited to the value of the share. The difference between an s.r.o. and an a.s. is that an a.s. can easily transfer shares to other persons without having to amend the articles of association.

- v.o.s. – *věřejná obchodní společnost* – general uniform company. The partners' liabilities are not limited to the investment but to all properties.
- k.s. – *komanditní společnost* – in which some partners have limited liability and some have unlimited.

Forming a Company in the Czech Republic

The laws on setting up a company are so complex and change so often that to give the entire details here would be a waste of time. Here are the basics:

- You must sign an article of association through a lawyer here and you must have a separate, official notary seal.
- You must get a trade license. Take the articles of association with the stamp of approval of the seat of the company, with all relevant diplomas and documents, to your district office: *Živnostenský odbor Obvodního úřadu.*
- Register the company at court. For this, submit: (a) the article of association; (b) the trade license; (c) the long-stay permit if the managing director is foreign; (d) a registered lease contract for the seat of the company; (e) a sworn affidavit from the investor that he will put the investment into the bank as soon as he is registered in court; and (f) an application to register at the court.

Setting up a Branch of an International Company

The regulations for setting up a branch office of an international company are different, as this is not creating a company, but expanding a company which has already legally established itself in another country or countries. A legal representative (managing director, etc.) of the company must arrange a founding deed in front of a notary, then go through different channels to establish the branch office.

Commercial Leasing

The laws regarding leasing of office space are generally the same as those for residential property (see above), although the lease of commercial space falls under a different law.

For information on leasing office space, you will need to go through a reputable real estate agency. Prime central office space in Prague rents for approximately 50–75 DM per square metre per month; prime retail space goes for roughly 100–200 DM per square meter per month. Out of centre rents are of course cheaper (approx. 20 DM psm and up per month).

Foreigners still face restrictions on owning property, though these laws are always changing. Contact a real estate agency for the latest information.

SCHOOLS

If you have children, you will of course want to find good schools for them in a language they will understand. Only the very youngest children have the innate capacity to pick up languages; therefore any children over the age of about five will need to attend a private international school. If you do have very young children, and you plan to stay more a year or more, you can do your child an enormous favour by sending him or her to a Czech nursery school (*mateřská škola*). Young children are always quick to adapt, and you'll be amazed and even embarrassed to hear your five-year-old speaking Czech after a few months. One acquaintance of mine has a daughter who went to *mateřská skola* for two years: her Czech is near-fluent, and her parents actually learn vocabulary from her! Nursery schools in general are very good, and after-school day care is usually provided if both parents work.

If you are interested in sending your child to a regular Czech public school, contact the office *(školský úřad)* of the school district in which you live.

International Schools

If your children are over the age of about five, you'll have to send them to an international school, of which there are several excellent (if expensive) ones in Prague, accredited by American, British, and other countries' school systems. It is important to contact these schools ahead of time as applications can be lengthy processes due to ever-increasing demand.

The International School of Prague is housed in a new complex in Prague 6-Nebušice to accommodate all grade levels. It operates under the auspices of the US Embassy and follows an American school curriculum. The nursery school covers ages 4–7, elementary school from US grades 3–6, and the secondary school includes grade levels 7–12, with a High School diploma accredited by the Middle States Association of US High Schools. Contact the school for applications at Mylnerovka 2, Praha 6, tel. 9004 9517 or 9005 2710.

The British International School of Prague offers nursery and primary education for children up to age 13. There are two locations of infants' schools, one in Prague 4 and one in Prague 6, plus a junior school located in Prague 2. Students can continue on to a joint Czech–British school (below). Contact the school's central offices at Belgická 25, 12 000 Praha 2, tel. 25 68 50, fax 2424 7025.

The English College in Prague is a separate institution, though linked with the British International School. Located in Prague 9 – Vysočany (near metro station Českomoravská), the school offers regular British secondary school curriculum (ages 14–18) leading to the International General Certificate of Secondary Education and the International Baccalaureate upon graduation. Contact the principal at Sokolovská 320, Praha 9, tel. 6631 0945, extension 206 (if a Czech answers the central, ask for *linka dvě stě šest*).

The French International School in Prague offers a French curriculum for pupils aged 3-18, in three separate schools. A French Maturité Baccalaureate is awarded to graduating seniors. The address is Krupkovo náměstí 1, Praha 6, tel. 32 28 72.

There is also an Austrian school in Prague, offering courses to Czechs and native German speakers who speak Czech. For information on both, contact them at Drtínová 3, Praha 5, tel. 54 32 53, 301 1725, or 880 375.

There are further opportunities for natives of Bulgaria (Pod Kaštany 14, Praha 6, tel. 37 30 66 or 38 12 70), Indonesia (Pod Kaštany 24, tel. 37 38 30), Poland (Sokolská 6, tel. 242 611 26), Libya (Bubenečská 59, Prague 6, tel. 311 8221), and Russia (Krupkovo náměstí 1, Praha 6, tel. 37 05 45).

PETS

If you are bringing your pet with you, you must have a certificate of health, which you obtain from your veterinarian at home – you must also have an animal passport with its photo!

Czech vets are excellent, inexpensive, and can be found in the Yellow Pages under *Veterináři*. Finding a vet that speaks English, however, may be a different story. Ask your embassy for suggestions.

Be aware that some landlords do not want tenants to have pets, although there is no official regulation about this. Czechs themselves are great dog lovers, and you always see dachshunds, schnausers and German shepherds in every park and metro. Czechs have an amusing habit of carrying small dogs in bags on the metro – this saves the ticket price for children and animals.

MONEY

The Czech unit of currency is the Czech crown *(Česká koruna)*, abbreviated as Kč, and broken down into hellers *(haléře)*. Crown notes come in denominations of 20, 50, 100, 200, 500, 1000, 2000, and 5000 Kč. Coins come in denominations of 0.10, 0.20, 0.50, 1, 2, 5, 10, 20, and 50 Kč.

The crown has been floating on money markets since early 1990, and has remained remarkably stable the past four years. It is tagged to the US dollar and the Deutsche Mark. The crown became almost fully convertible in October 1995. Czechs are permitted to exchange any amount of crowns into any other currency, while foreigners must provide exchange receipts if they want to change more than 5000 Kč back into foreign currency.

Czech banks and shops do not honour personal cheques. Credit cards are gaining wider acceptance; most shops or restaurants and all banks which deal with Western clients will accept American Express, MasterCard, Visa, or Eurocard. There are several bank ATMs which honour the above cards as well as Czech-bank issued debit cards.

Banking

Banks underwent fundamental change during the early 1990s, along with the very economy on which they operated. There still exist some serious problems, which will take several years yet to clear up, but as the pace of change here is so fast, it will not be long before Czech banking falls into line with with the rest of Europe. But currently the Czech financial sector lacks some of the mechanisms and resources to perform what would be considered full banking services in the West, though as everything here, it's improving. The system in general is hindered by underdeveloped computerisation and telecommunications, so systems of credit and information integration are not yet fully established. My bank still uses microfiche and filing cabinets to process transactions – immensely inefficient and frustrating!

Despite these pitfalls, it is possible to obtain brokerage and investment advice, loans, and underwriting services, as well as standard commercial transactions. New banks have emerged to offer various service specialisations, and several foreign banks now have branch offices here, while the older monoliths, Komerční Banka and Česká Spořitelna, are expanding and refining services.

Personal and Business Accounts

It is not difficult to open a savings account in a Czech bank for personal or business use—and the use of local ATM cards is becoming more common. Interest rates in standard savings accounts hover at around the 2% to 3% mark, while time deposits gain interest of between 6% to 16% depending on length of deposit. All you need to open an account in a Czech bank is your passport. Still, be ready for a few frustrations here and there: it can take several days until your account is functioning properly, and you must apply for an ATM card, which then takes over a month to be issued. The largest Czech banks include Česká Spořitelna, Československá Obchodní Banka, Ecoagrobanka, Investiční Banka, Komerční Banka, and Živnostenská Banka.

Foreign Banks

Foreign banks in the Czech Republic function as representative offices or branches, and they face limitations on accounts openings and on lending. The role of foreign banks is to serve their clients in Prague, of course, but also, for the time being at least, to complement or fill-in for services not yet undertaken by Czech banks. They can offer advice and handle transactions through the authorisation of the parent bank, and they are useful in dealing with transactions with Western clients. Foreign banks in operation include ABN-AMRO Bank, Bank Austria, Bankers Trust, Bayerische Vereinsbank, BNP Dresdner Bank, Citibank, Commerzbank, Creditanstalt, CS First Boston, Hypobank, and ING Bank.

TAXATION

Many people consider taxation a good reason to live abroad, as most do not have to pay taxes at home when not conducting business there. Foreigners living in the Czech Republic are responsible for paying Czech taxes, though, unless working under their embassy.

Whether you work as a freelance entrepreneur or as an employee of a Czech legal entity, you are required to pay income tax, which is graded. All legally employed workers pay social insurance, health insurance, and a percentage of the remaining gross income, which can work out to quite a high figure. If you work independently, you must file for and pay taxes yourself – contact an accountant for the help you will certainly need. If you are an employee of a Czech company, your taxes will be automatically deducted from your pay, but check with your company's accounting department nonetheless to make sure you face no further tax payments.

Corporate taxes are a whopping 41% – part of the reason for the state's economic success. There are now provisions for tax deductions of up to 30% for certain legally-resident foreigners.

The state value added tax (VAT) is presently 22% on all goods, including food. This is eventually expected to fall in line with Western

Europe's standard 19%. All prices quoted in shops, restaurants etc. include VAT. Service industries face a tax of 5%.

INSURANCE

As with banks, the insurance sector is undergoing fundamental change, and as with banks, the system is deficient in basic capital and facilities. The former giant Česká Pojišt'ovna has evolved into the market leader, offering life insurance, personal property and liability insurance, industrial insurance, agricultural insurance, and international insurance. Such services are available to foreigners legally living and working in Prague, though most expats prefer to arrange personal insurance through their agent at home, or opt for one of the foreign companies operating in Prague. For business insurance, consult with one of the foreign companies listed below, whose numbers and services are ever-expanding.

Foreign insurance firms operating in the Czech Republic include Allianz, Austria-Collegialitüt, First American-Czech Insurance Company, Goather Versicherengen, Harris and Dixon, Marsh and McLennan, Minet, and Nationale Nederlanden.

HEALTH

It is a good idea to have a complete physical exam before you come, though the long-stay authorities no longer have health requirements included in their entrance requirements.

The Czech Republic is overall a very healthy country in which to travel and live: standards of cleanliness and hygiene are high, except for the poor air quality in cities which you can't avoid in winter. Health care is quite good and still inexpensive, though this latter fact is a bone of contention in the current political agenda: doctor's salaries are remarkably low, and the health care industry is ripe for reform.

Illnesses and emergencies can often be treated by English-speaking Czech doctors, many of whom have studied and worked in Western countries.

Foreigners in Prague have a few options for medical care:

The First Medical Clinic of Prague, at Vyšehradská 35, Prague 2, is a regular Czech health clinic with good English-speaking doctors. They charge 650 Kč for a visit (no foreign insurance policies accepted) and can refer you to specialised treatment or hospital stays. The clinic is open from 7am–5pm, Monday to Friday, though it's best to call for an appointment, tel. 292 286. Its 24-hour emergency hotline is 0601 225 050.

Nearby is the Emergency First Aid Clinic of the Charles University, at Karlovo náměstí 32, tel. 2490 4111, open daily 7am–4pm; again, you pay for services directly.

There is a similar clinic called the Canadian Medical Centre, at Veleslavínská 1/30, Prague 6, tel. 316 5519, or 0601 225 050 after hours, operated by Canadian doctors and thus charging higher fees. They do accept international insurance policies, however.

Competing with them is the American Medical Centre, staffed by American and Czech doctors and nurses, at Janovského 48, Prague 7, tel. 807 756 or 877 793. Hours are Monday to Friday 8.30 am–6 pm. They offer all medical and dental services, foreign insurance policies are accepted, and they have their own pharmacy.

There is a special department for foreigners at the hospital Nemocnice Na Homolce, Roentgenova 2, Prague 5, with full services and English-speaking doctors on call 24 hours a day, experienced in all matters of health service, including arranging insurance with your provider at home. This is Prague's main hospital. Call 5292 2146 or 5292 2191 for an appointment.

For high quality gynaecological care, contact the Meda Women's Clinic in Bulovka Hospital, Budínova 2, Praha 8. The phone numbers are 6608 3239 or 6608 3268.

For emergency dental care, contact the clinic at Vladislavova 22 in Praha 1, tel. 2422 7663. Dentists are noted to be very good, and services fall under general health insurance if you have your long-stay permit.

Outside of Prague, you'll have to rely on the local hospital or clinic, easily located in the local directories.

Health Insurance

If you have a long-stay permit, you are covered by state health insurance – you're paying for it out of your monthly or yearly taxes. Doctor's visits require no payment, though you must show your health insurance card, which you will be issued after obtaining your long-stay permit. Prescription drugs are also covered, in part. Present your doctor's prescription note at a pharmacy and you'll be charged pleasantly low amounts for medication.

If you are not on Czech health insurance, you had better obtain an international insurance policy. Your provider at home can help you arrange this, or can at least refer you to other companies that will. For a regular doctor's visit, you are expected to pay the fee as charged (it is quite reasonable), then claim reimbursement from your insurance company at home. For more serious (and hence, expensive) medical treatments, you will have to arrange something between your hospital and your insurance company. For such serious problems as surgery, you may feel more comfortable at home.

The following provide a broad range of comprehensive service; contact them for a brochure:

- Patriot International, International Medical Group, Inc., 135 N. Pennsylvania, Suite 1700, Indianapolis, IN, 46204, USA.
- International Health Insurance Danmark, 8 Palaegade, DK-1261, Copenhagen K, Denmark, tel. +45 33 15 30 99, fax. +45 33 32 25 60.

Many foreigners living in Prague prefer to retain Western policies and receive treatment from Western doctors working here. In some cases this is prudent, though the Czech health care system is perfectly adequate.

Pharmaceuticals

Most any medication you need is available from pharmacies here, though you will not likely find the same brand names. Most Czech-made medicines are equally effective, and foreign-made products are usually available. Specific brands such as Tylenol and Pepto Bismal are not readily available, so if you have a fondness for these particular drugs, bring a supply with you. Similarly, if you are on specific medication, be sure to bring a stock with you, as the exact same product may not be available.

Most medications beyond aspirin and vitamins require a doctor's prescription, so if you are accustomed to buying antihistimines or sleeping pills over the counter, be forewarned that you can't do so here.

CRIME AND SECURITY

The Czech Republic certainly does not feel like a dangerous place, though statistics throughout the country indicate that rates of theft and violent crime are rising dramatically. Overall, however, it is quite safe to take a late metro or tram home, or to walk through town alone at night.

The most rampant crimes are pickpocketing and car theft. Especially in touristy areas of Prague, and especially in summer, slippery fingers are something to worry about. Keep your bags close to your body, carry money in a secure money belt, or in a wallet in your front pocket or jacket pocket, and be especially wary of crowds. It's easy to imagine tourists wowed by the city being an easy target for clever thieves. Groups of gypsies are watched with a particularly keen eye by locals.

Car theft has become a serious issue of late, and most car owners now secure their vehicle with a steering wheel clamp. Flashy Mercedes and BMWs are an obvious target, though the domestically produced Škoda is equally desirable – with close to 75% of the cars on the road being made by Škoda, it's quite easy for them to disappear into the crowd.

The drug trade is picking up force, and there's a lot of talk in the news about changing the drug laws, which currently allow a person to possess a small amount of marijuana for personal use. Of course, it's officially illegal to sell or buy any drugs, and the police have succeeded in making some impressive raids on cocaine and locally produced Pervitin dealers.

171

PROSTITUTION

Prostitution is a business here as anywhere, and, like the possession of drugs, it falls into a sort of grey-market status. The country does have its share of *bordely* (brothels), which operate legally as massage parlours and sex shops – any other activity that occurs is discreet and for the most part tolerated by the police. Street walkers are abundant around the Wenceslas Square area in Prague nightly, and, surprisingly, along the highways leading to the German borders. It's quite a site: leather skirted women sitting on guard rails in full daylight, who make a living off Germans crossing the border for a couple hours!

The number of AIDS cases is increasing, though the figures are still very low.

THE EXPATRIATE COMMUNITY

The expatriate community in Prague merits a special section of its own here. Somehow Prague has been a magnet for backpackers and businesspeople ever since 1990, especially amongst Americans. It is estimated that up to 30,000 Americans now live in Prague, and it's easy to believe if you happen to frequent any of the bookstores, restaurants, clubs, and even laundromats haunted by these visitors from the West.

To be quite honest, I avoid such establishments as much as possible. Sure, they are a great place to meet people of similar interests and experiences (getting together to harp on culture shock topics is a prime motivator in many people's social lives here), but it becomes a pit that swallows you up – by limiting your contact with Czechs, you miss out on what is one of the most critical factors in experiencing and enjoying your stay abroad. As the owner of one local expat dive told me, "Business is great, but we've created a monster." Several such places did serve a very useful function back in 1992 or so when they first appeared – the city was still very much lost in time, and for those who were used to having burgers, burritos, bookstores, and fellow patrons who speak the same language as you, it was hard to stay away.

A MAGNET FOR BACK PACKERS

This purpose has largely been eliminated lately, as more and more eating, drinking, and socialising establishments owned by Czechs have opened up that offer greater variety and quality than what was available before. (I've listed several expatriate gathering points in the back of the book).

So you're quite lucky in that life here is now almost on par with the rest of western Europe in terms of comfort and convenience; though on the other hand, the sense of daring and adventure has been reduced. Back in the early 1990s (oh so long ago), daily life was still a bit of a challenge: everything was grey, standards and variety of goods available was much lower than now, and for many foreigners relocating here, the country was exotic and exciting in many ways. Many (myself included) were charmed by the frozen-in-time feel to the place, kind of a back-to-the-future nostalgia which is rapidly disappearing.

Many of the first visitors in the country were backpackers who got caught up in the charm (and cheap beer) of Prague, and ended up spending months hanging out on Charles Bridge, learning Czech, and mingling with the locals. At the same time, businesses jumped in, using Prague as the base not only for their Czech, but in many cases for their entire east Europe operations, and Western managers came in droves to set up shop and train Czechs. Now that many Czechs are well qualified to operate branch offices of foreign firms, some managers are leaving; though with so many more companies expanding to Prague, the numbers of incoming expatriates remains steady.

Still, it seems extraordinary that so many foreigners have chosen to live in Prague. Part of the reason is simple: this is a gorgeous city with a captivating atmosphere, and Czechs are a wonderful people once you get to know them. You'll never tire of walking around the city on a quiet weekend, or going to concerts and pubs, or discovering different parts of the country, and even though it will take a bit of effort, you'll find the Czech people an irresistibly funny and friendly lot. In more practical terms, there are so many opportunities in the Czech Republic, and especially in Prague, that many people find themselves either experiencing success in their current occupation, and therefore wanting to stay for economic reasons, or coming across new and exciting prospects while here.

GOING HOME – CULTURE SHOCK IN REVERSE

Strange as it seems, going back home after living abroad is often much more difficult than moving abroad in the first place. You expect things to be different and confusing when you go elsewhere, but coming home should be so easy and natural, right? Wrong.

While you've been away, you've had experiences which could never have happened at home – and you've grown immeasurably from them. Meanwhile, your friends and colleagues have gone through changes of their own, which you haven't been a part of. It takes time to get back into the swing of things, and you're apt to find that once you do so, it lacks the day-to-day excitement of living in a different culture. Having gotten to know a different part of the world, and hence expanded your horizons, home will not quite feel like the home it used to be.

So just as you go through periods of depression and frustration when you live abroad, you unwittingly do the same upon your return, and it's even more 'shocking' because you feel a stranger in your own home. Again, let things unwind on their own, think positively about all you've learned while you were away, and realise that reverse culture shock – re-adapting to home life – is as natural as adjusting to a foreign culture in the first place.

— Chapter Nine —

ENTERTAINMENT AND CULTURE

THE ARTS IN THE CZECH LANDS

Throughout its history, much of the architectural development of the Czech nation was the result of the work of foreign masters commissioned by kings and nobility. These served to bring the general movements to Czech artists, who then produced their own work within the style. Czech painters, sculptors, composers, and writers similarly did not begin any trends of their own, rather they were influenced by Continental movements, to which they added personal and national elements. A few Czechs reached international stature through the years, but it wasn't until the 19th century and the National Revival that Czech artists really came into their own.

During the Hapsburg era, a host of German, Austrian, and Italian artists came to the Czech lands to bring the age of the Baroque to flower. Some of the greatest names of this era spent substantial portions of their careers in Prague, and much of their work is still standing. Bavarian architect Christoph Dientzenhofer and his son

Kilian Ignaz (born in Prague) designed dozens of churches in the capital city and around the country. Prominent sculptors include Matthias Braun, an imported Austrian, and the native-born Ferdinand Maxmilian Brokof. One particular feature of the Baroque that emerged in the Czech lands is the peculiar semi-onion-dome steeple which sits atop literally hundreds of churches across the country. This is in fact a common feature of the Baroque in central Europe, most prominently on display in this country.

It is curious to note the ties that the arts have had with politics in the Czech lands, particularly in the past two centuries. In the 19th century Czech art began to take on a personality of its own, and the growth of nationalism through the arts had enormous consequence on political developments into the following century. Much of the 20th century has been marked by painful political oppression, which created in the artistic underworld a sentiment of both despair and hope which has been so eloquently brought out especially by novelists of the 1960s and 70s.

THE NATIONAL REVIVAL

During the late 19th century, Czech artists and thinkers began a movement which came to be known as the National Revival *(Narodní obrození)*. Three hundred odd years of Austrian rule weighed heavily on the intellectual spirit, and a sense of national awakening, or reawakening, had begun to snowball into a political movement by the end of the century.

There are several explanations for the rise of this movement. This was the Romantic era in the arts, a time when an appreciation for natural beauty, along with a new awareness of folk elements, produced an enthusiastic output of literary and musical material. In addition, the Industrial Revolution during this century brought great numbers of Czechs from the countryside into cities to work in factories, thereby condensing Czech populations in these cities which up to this point had substantial populations of Germans and Austrians.

The revival was 'launched' by intellectuals, whose spiritual leader was the politician and writer Frantiček Palacky. A staunch supporter of the emerging pan-Slavic movement, Palacky wrote his *History of the Czech Nation in Bohemia and Moravia* in 1836, a landmark work that was instrumental in creating a sense of national awareness and pride, and its contents helped give rise to a plethora of artistic developments in the succeeding decades.

Very few of the writers, composers, and artists of the time are well known internationally, but this fact only serves to increase their endearment to the Czechs. The poets Karel Hynek Mácha and Božena Němcová are true Romantics, writing of country themes, love, and death. Alois Jirásek is famed for his collection of Czech folk tales, while Jan Neruda is similarly held in high regard for his touching stories of life in Prague's Malá Strana district.

Similarly, much of the music that comes from this time follows the Romantic inclination. Bedřich Smetana is the darling of Czech composition, particularly for his epic work *Má Vlast (My Country)*, incorporating the mythology and sonorities of the Bohemian country-side into a large scale symphonic poem. Antonín Dvořák is perhaps better known throughout the music world; his intricate and powerful works in nearly all genres incorporate a strong folk element into what has been described as an irrepressible positiveness.

Architecture soon followed suit, and in Prague, the construction of the National Theatre, National Museum, and the Rudolfinum concert hall were landmark achievements. Funding for these enormous projects came literally from the pockets of the locals, and their establishment as centres of Czech theatrical, musical, and cultural expression and concentration rendered them important showpieces. Of equal symbolic importance was the progress taken to finally complete the Cathedral of St. Vitus, begun in 929 by the nation's patron saint, Václav.

By the end of the 19th century, these influences had begun to forge a political movement. With the onset of World War I and the political

177

rise of Tomáš G. Masaryk, Czech intellectuals pushed for an independence which was finally gained in 1918.

THE 20TH CENTURY

Czech culture in the 20th century takes in all the fits and starts of this schizophrenic time, expounding them with the suppressed energy of a proud nation. Emerging from the 400 year hold of the Austro-Hungarian Empire into a mere 20 years of freedom, only to be knocked down by crushing back-to-back Nazi and Communist rule, the country's artistic output demonstrates the anguish and stagnation of repressed pride. This century has produced an oddly steady series of twisted, at times subversive, artists which somehow retain a playful, typically Czech sceptical attitude toward existence.

In the field of architecture, the art-nouveau and secessionist periods brought flowery and angular commercial and residential palaces into streetscapes. Cubism caught on here like nowhere else; the Czech lands are one of the only places in the world where cubist architecture went beyond the design stage and into real buildings. The basic principle of cubism is to rebel against such fundamental architectural features as surface uniformity – the country's cubist buildings utilise new spatial dimensions in a truly revolutionary creation: triangular window edgings, jutting corners, and oval staircases predominate.

Sculpture became acutely expressive at this time—Czech artists such as František Bílek and Jan Štursa created particularly moving images out of wood and bronze, and their work is quite well regarded within their respective circles. The best known Czech painter of this era is undoubtedly Alfons Mucha, who made a living in Paris for much of his life off his art-nouveau graphic art posters, though he returned home toward the end of his life to produce a series of epic paintings on Slavic history and mythology.

Twentieth century Czech composers are numerous and their output voluminous. Composers such as Leoš Janáček (who in fact belonged to both the 19th century Romantic era and the 20th century impressionist and expressionist movements), Bohuslav Martinů, and Vitězslav Novák are fiery, emotional, and at times incoherent. Where form begins to dissipate in many of their works, raw energy bursts forth.

Perhaps the most tangible expression of the tumultuous 20th century in this country is to be found in the wealth of superb literature, which would not have come into existence were it not for such destructive external forces. One of the first great works of this century's fiction is *The Good Soldier Schweik*, written (largely under a drunken stupor) by Jaroslav Hašek in the midst of the collapse of the Hapsburg Empire during World War I.

Although Franz Kafka spent his entire life in Prague, he was a member of the German community, and so has no real home in today's Czech society – a cruelly fitting end to this dark, schizophrenic novelist. His works are often set in a city which could be Prague, with characters that could be typical government officials of the time, and it's the very acuteness of his absurdly vague settings that make him so popular, yet to consider Kafka Czech is a fallacy.

Writers under the Communist era faced severe censorship and risked imprisonment for speaking the truth. This of course only encouraged them more, and a generation of excellent playwrights and novelists emerged in the 1960s that produced some truly outstanding works of subtle social commentary. Their means of expression in fact were very carefully conveyed, and a handful of the most challenging writers were kept on authorities' blacklists for years. Some, in fact were able to leave the country in 1968: Milan Kundera left for Paris, Josef Škvorecký immigrated to Canada, and film-maker Miloš Forman moved to the US. Meanwhile Ivan Klíma, Bohumil Hrabal, and Václav Havel, among others, endured through the 1980s; their perseverance is a source of admiration and inspiration.

The central theme in most works by these writers is that of human relations, particularly in the scope of living under oppression.

Škvorecky's *The Engineer of Human Souls* is a particularly insightful and poignant collage of stories about life under Nazism and Communism, presenting many dark images, yet related in a typically casual air of seeming indifference. Kundera is internationally recognised as one of the finest living novelists. He, like Hrabal, incorporates images of the Czech countryside and people into his often insightful, often funny, and often sexually deviant stories. Klíma on the other hand sheds a more realistic and depressing light on the reality of living under an oppressive regime, while Havel's writing is divided between absurdist theatre and direct commentary in essay form on the immense frustrations and injustices of the Communist state. Refer to the reading list at the back of this book for a more complete rundown of individual works of these writers.

CONCERT LIFE

Prague has a never ending run of top quality concerts, operas, ballet, theatre, and club shows. Tickets for most are still remarkably cheap, though not at the expense of quality – the Czech Philharmonic is internationally regarded as an excellent symphony orchestra, and the city's numerous theatres and concert halls draw top names from around the world. Many of the performance halls in the city are architectural showpieces in their own right – the National Theatre, Estates Theatre, and Rudolfinum Concert Hall in particular are spectacular venues in which to absorb the arts.

Information on shows can be obtained from the listings in the weekly newspaper *The Prague Post*, or from the signs posted around town. If you're a dedicated follower of classical music, theatre, or dance, stop by the box offices of the major halls and pick up a monthly program. It is usually possible to purchase tickets at the door, though stopping by the ticket office a day or two before the show is always safer. It is also possible to purchase season tickets, or series of tickets: both the Prague Symphony Orchestra (FOK) and the Czech Philharmonic, for example, run what they call concert cycles, such as the

Rudolfinum Concert Hall – home of the Czech Philharmonic, and an example of architecture during the National Revival.

cycle of contemporary music, the cycle of the piano repertoire, and various orchestral series. There is usually one concert a month within each cycle, and the savings are substantial.

THEATRES

Prague has three wonderful theatres/opera houses, all recently restored to their former 18th and 19th century glory.

- The National Theatre *(Národní divadlo),* built in 1881 only to be immediately burned down and subsequently rebuilt with contributions from private citizens, is a showcase for operas and plays. It is located at the corner of Národní street and the river.
- The Estates Theatre *(Stavovské divadlo),* formerly *Tylovo divadlo* – where Mozart conducted the premier of *Don Giovanni,* located at the corner of Železná and Rytířská streets in Old Town, was restored in 1991, and is a gorgeous venue for opera, theatre, and ballet.

- The State Opera House *(Státní opera),* also known as *Smetanovo divadlo*, is Prague's third great theatre/opera house, located just between the museum and the main train station on Wilsonovo Street. It looks a bit out of place with cars whizzing past, but it is a glorious hall.

Concert Halls

In addition to the theatres above, Prague has two major concert halls and several smaller ones, all with programs several times a week.

- *Rudolfinum*, with the grand *Dvořákova síň* hall, remodelled in 1990, is home to the Czech Philharmonic and frequently hosts visiting symphonies and instrumental soloists. Monthly and yearly schedules are available at the ticket office on the side of the building at náměstí Jana Palacha, Prague 1.
- *Smetanova síň*, in the Municipal House *(Obecní dům)* at náměstí Republiky is now open—a truly marvellous Art Nouveau building. Home to the Prague Symphony Orchestra, the hall is another popular concert venue. Monthly and yearly schedules are available at the FOK ticket office, housed at the back of the building.

There are dozens of smaller concert and theatre venues dotted around the city, including many churches and small halls.

Jazz, Rock, and Dance Clubs

Jazz, rock, and dance clubs are also very popular – if you don't have tickets for bigger-draw shows in advance, it will be difficult to get in. For walk-in-off-the-street clubs, you will probably want to get there early – by about 9 pm, to be sure you get a seat.

Jazz has a small but dedicated following. In addition, there are some great Czech bands playing everything from pop to bluegrass, to reggae to thrash metal. Check the weekly papers or program guides for information on venues and programs.

Major rock shows have hit Prague, as the city becomes a regular for concert tours. Several big name rock bands who have played Prague in recent years include the Rolling Stones, Guns n Roses, Michael Jackson, REM, ZZ Top, and Tracy Chapman, among others.

Cafes and Teashops

In addition to the endless selection of pubs, Prague has several good cafes *(kavárna)* and tea shops *(čajovna)*. Somehow the standard European cafe hasn't quite established itself in Prague, so the city doesn't have quite the cafe culture that cities such as Paris or Milan do. As everything in this fine city, though, it's getting better.

Although tea is not a culturally rooted phenomenon here as it is elsewhere, Prague has a number of delightful teashops.

Bookstores

For English-speakers, there are a few bookstores in Prague with a good selection.

- The Globe, Janovského 14, Holešovice, is an expat institution, with lots of new and used books and a popular cafe frequented by hip young travellers and 'writers.' It draws a lot of attention, and the atmosphere can sometimes be stifling.
- U Knihomola, Mánesova 79, Vínohrady, is more classy, with a greater variety of books on art history, architecture, travel, cooking, and so on.
- Bohemia Ventures, náměstí Jana Palacha 2, (in the Philosophy Faculty building of Charles University), Old Town, has a decent selection of novels as well as textbooks and dictionaries.
- Big Ben Bookshop, Malá Štupartská, Old Town, is similarly well-stocked.

Foreign Cultural Centres

The following cultural centres are all linked with their embassies, with the purpose of spreading their nation's culture and customs to the

183

local population. They also serve as magnets for homesick foreign nationals with their libraries and programs. If your nationality is not represented below, you can contact your embassy to find information about cultural and social events.

- The Austrian Embassy has a small cultural department at Viktora Huga 10, Prague 5, Smíchov, tel. 2451 1667
- The British Council, Národní 10, New Town, tel. 2491 2179, has books, films, current newspapers and magazines, and lectures.
- The French Institute, Štěpánská 35, New Town, 2421 4032, is an excellent cultural centre for anyone interested in France, with a library, gallery, cafe, theatre, language courses, and regular films.
- The Goethe Institute, Masarykova nábřeží 32, New Town, tel. 2491 5725, is a centre of German culture, with language courses, a library, films and presentations.
- The Hungarian Cultural Centre is at Rytířská 25-27 in Old Town, tel. 2422 2424
- The Italian Cultural Centre and Library, Šporkova 14, Malá Strana, tel. 2451 0204, offers regular films and get-togethers.
- There is a small Polish Institute at Václavské náměstí 49, tel. 2422 8722, with occasional exhibitions, films, and a shop.
- The Slovak Cultural Centre, at Purkyňova 53/4, tel. 2491 5629, is a good source of information on what was recently the other part of Czechoslovakia.
- The US Embassy has a cultural centre and library at Hybernská 7 near náměstí Republiky (tel. 2423 1085), with a library containing books by American authors, magazines and newspapers; cultural programs and occasional exhibitions also on offer.

MOVIES

The Czech film industry is remarkably active, considering how small the country is and how many American films flood the cinemas these days. Hollywood films are indeed very popular, arriving some two to six months after their premieres in the States. Nearly all foreign films are shown in their original language with subtitles in Czech, though movies are occasionally dubbed – check this before you buy tickets.

The film studio AB Barrandov releases new films regularly, many of which are of exceptional quality, and many of which tend toward the cerebral. Czechs seem to like films that invoke a response and pose a question or two. One popular recent film was an adaptation of a well loved 19th century collection of stories of Prague's Malá Strana district, in this version reset to the 1980s. The stories centre around a favourite local pub, where neighbours congregate to chat, to commiserate, to question life, and to disappear from what Communism has created. Unfortunately for most of us, Czech films only very rarely have English subtitles.

SPORTS AND LEISURE

Hockey and football (soccer) are the two national sports, and both national teams are among the best in Europe. Czech hockey in particular has produced an astounding number of topnotch players – dozens play professionally in the most prestigious leagues in North America and Europe; they won the 1996 world championships and the Olympic team is always a medal contender. Getting tickets to hockey and football matches is rarely a problem, except for the big international events.

Czechoslovakia produced two of the 1980s' top tennis players – Martina Navrátilová and Ivan Lendl – though both moved to the US during their careers. The tradition continues today, though with all this success, tennis is oddly not a popular spectator sport at all.

As health-consciousness picks up steam, fitness centres are becoming more and more popular. Prague especially has lots of new weight training centres, aerobics classes, indoor swimming pools, and so on. Major hotels all have fitness centres open to the public. Even squash is catching on – in Prague there are two squash centres operated by Esquo at the Strahov stadium complex (tel. 357 093).

185

Everyone enjoys the outdoors in all seasons, whether it's lounging around the cottage, gardening, or engaging in more strenuous activities. The countryside is well-patterned with hiking trails, which often become cross-country ski trails in winter. Downhill skiing is also popular, with the slopes in the Krkonoše mountains offering the best runs. There are adequate facilities for equipment rental both in Prague and in the mountains. Ice skating on frozen ponds is a common activity too.

In summer, everyone heads off to one of the country's rivers for canoe float trips. *Jdu na vodě* – "I'm going to the water" – is a common reason to take a few days off, and it's great fun to just float down a river and pitch a tent. It's also possible to rent rowboats on the Vltava in Prague, or to hop aboard a river cruise. Fishing and hunting are common pursuits as well.

Billiards and table tennis are popular indoor activities.

Skating and hockey are popular pastimes – even in the grey high-rise suburbs local residents take advantage of the outdoors.

CULTURAL AND TRADITIONAL CALENDAR EVENTS

Czechs take a very festive approach toward everyday life, whether it's leaving work early, celebrating someone's name day, going to the pub for the evening, or participating in one of the numerous festivals that mark the calendar at regular intervals. Traditional cultural events make up an important part of the social calendar, and organised festivals are also an integral part of Czech social life. Here's a sampling of the fun to be had, by season – some official, some just generally observed.

Spring

Easter Monday. Don't forget this is not a religious nation, so Easter Sunday is merely the middle day in a three-day weekend. Easter Monday is the first official day off since January 1, so it comes as a welcome respite. Czechs still take part in an amusing tradition, which some find shocking: my first year in Prague was a surprise introduction to it. I was an English teacher at a Czech primary school, and on the Friday before the Easter weekend as I walked down the corridor to class, a group of my giggling 10-year-old girls ran up to me with sticks in their hands, then dutifully formed a line in front of me – and bent over as if to be spanked! I looked over, disconcerted, at a colleague, who motioned that I should indeed administer a whipping. In the US I would likely lose my job over this, so I really hesitated, but a crowd had formed by now, urging me on. So I cautiously lifted the stick and let it fall gently on the upturned behind of the first in line, at which point everyone shouted, "Harder! Harder!" I was mystified. It turns out this is part of an age-old belief that when young girls are whipped with birch sticks on Easter Monday, they will be guaranteed fertility from the sapling branches. Receiving it from a baffled American seemed to be extra promising.

The Burning of the Witches, or *čarodějnice*, on April 30, is a pagan tradition of sorts in which everyone must build a witch out of straw and old clothes, then burn it on a bonfire in their backyard in order to exorcise the land of evil spirits, which are said to rise on the eve of May Day. City folk tend to guffaw at the tradition, though in the country it's a great excuse to roast sausages outdoors.

The Prague Spring International Music Festival is a highly-acclaimed festival of classical music, running for three weeks from May 12 to June 2. The festival starts on the day of composer Bedřich Smetana's death, and naturally opens with a performance of his nationalist work *Má Vlast (My Homeland)*, attended by the president; the final show is always a rousing performance of Beethoven's incomparable 9th Symphony. Throughout the three weeks there are several concerts daily, and you can choose from among series of orchestral performances, soloists, chamber groups, ancient music, and contemporary music.

There is also a prestigious competition held, for different instruments every year. The festival naturally attracts famous performers, which in recent years have included Sir Georg Solti, Vladimir Ashkenazy, and James Galway. Tickets are sometimes obtainable at the door, though you're more likely to succeed in getting tickets by going to the Prague Spring ticket office, located at Hellichova 18, Prague 1-Malá Strana. Better yet is to get a hold of the ticket order form, which is released in November (you can pick it up at most major theatre and concert hall box offices), and send in your ticket requests.

Summer

Summertime sees lots of folk festivals throughout the land. One of the most popular, which draws visitors and performers from as far away as Lithuania and Scotland, is the international folk festival held at Strážnice in south Moravia in the last weekend of June. Traditional music, dance, and crafts are on offer.

The outdoor folk museum at Rožnov pod Radhoštem in north Moravia is open all summer long.

Karlovy Vary has an international film festival starting the last weekend in June and running for eight days, drawing top name actors, actresses, and producers to the screenings. Prague began its own film festival in 1995, producing an almost bitter competition with Karlovy Vary. The Golden Golem festival, as it's called, is held every other year.

Český Krumlov hosts an international classical music festival in mid-August, not nearly as grand as the Prague Spring festival, but the location is charming nonetheless.

Autumn

There is yet another festival of classical music in Prague in September, appropriately named the Prague Autumn. This is a month-long series of classical music concerts of all genres, though again, not nearly as impressive as the spring version.

Folk traditions come alive again at this time, as this is harvest time. One of the most important crops is grapes, and Czechs have a special way of producing a sweet 'young' wine called *burčák*, which is drunk with abandon at weekend celebrations throughout wine country. Towns in north Bohemia, such as Litoměřice, host medieval and renaissance festivals concurrently, while Moravian towns such as Hodonín and Mikulov fest the fruity drink with barrels in the town square throughout late September and early October.

Meat is appropriately celebrated with a horrible pig slaughter, called *zabijačka*. The animal is strung up and gutted, and all body parts are used to make chops and sausages. *Jítrnice* is a particularly unhealthy, though delicious blood sausage. On a more mundane level, everyone heads into the forest to gather mushrooms in the fall.

Cross-country skiing is a popular winter sport and many people spend their holidays on the snow.

Winter

Christmas. Again, this is not really a religious day. Christmas is actually celebrated on the 24th, not the 25th as most elsewhere, and the entire proceeding is a bit different from what most are used to. On the evening of the 24th, families gather together for the traditional meal of fried carp and potato salad.

The entire Christmas season is festive and joyous, as stalls open up around city centres from early December to sell wreathes, wooden charms, and hot mulled wine, while nativity scenes and blacksmith shops add a touch of the olden days to the atmosphere. December 6 is St. Nicholas' Day, when jolly old St. Nick comes around to leave gifts for children – this is Santa Claus, three weeks early. Adults meanwhile turn it into a sort of Halloween and dress up as angels and devils and go out drinking. On the night of December 24, Jesus himself comes and leaves a second round of gifts for children under the tree – parents have to be crafty and sneak them there sometime during the meal, adding to the magic of discovery.

To lighten the heavy burden of a five-month winter, balls are held regularly throughout February and March. These can be anything from black-tie proms to 1930s big band shows to country/bluegrass hoedowns. It provides a nice (if usually drunken) pause in what is a dreary time of year.

Name Days (Svátek)

Every day on the calendar has a first name which is associated with it – these were originally days assigned to honour saints, though now every Czech name has its own day. In fact, Kafkaesque as it sounds, there exists a government office on names, which must be consulted if you choose to give your baby a name other than one of those on the calendar! Czechs rarely do this though, and therefore name days such as Jan, Josef, Jana, and Eva are exceedingly busy.

It is very important to be aware of your colleagues' and friends' name days – they are in fact almost a second birthday to Czechs. Offices often let loose at lunchtime or after work for a celebratory bottle. Flower shops run a brisk trade, and many post the day's name of honour on a billboard outside.

CULTURAL QUIZ

Now that your introduction to Czech culture is complete, all that remains is for you to experience it for yourself. A willingness to embrace Czech customs and a genuine interest in the people will take you a long way, but be patient in the initial stages as it takes time to adjust to any new social environment. The following questions will help test your new found knowledge and instincts about the country.

SITUATION ONE

You've just moved into your new flat and are eager to get to know your neighbours, though nobody seems to pay you any mind whatsoever when they see you in the hall. Do you:

A Get offended and ignore them too.

B Say hello and move on.

C Introduce yourself and try to draw them into conversation.

D Invite them in to your flat for a house-warming party and a get-to-know-you.

Comments

Although A is a natural response, remember that most Czechs simply keep to themselves. Saying hello to them may meet with a mumbled reply, though it will still take a while to establish any form of a relationship. After a few such meetings, recognition will set in and the ice may begin to melt. Inquiring into their lives too soon may be seen as probing, so gradual warm-up conversation pieces, such as comments on the weather, are your best way in. Option D, while it may be a common, friendly gesture in your own country, is far too personal here – it's a bit too close for comfort to enter someone's home if you aren't properly familiar with them. For now, B is the best answer, after which you can progress to C.

SITUATION TWO

You are in a pub after work with your new Czech colleagues. After a beer, the waiter comes around with another handful of mugs and your colleagues start to take in another round. You don't really want to drink, but you don't want to offend your colleagues by not taking part. Do you:

A Refuse the drink graciously and leave politely, saying you have another commitment

B Order coffee or water instead

C Drink on with them, seeing as this is an ice-breaking opportunity

Comments

Meeting after hours with colleagues is a great way to begin the friendly aspect of the relationship which is so important to Czechs. Furthermore, they tend to keep their social schedules flexible, particularly when it comes to meeting someone over a beer. To refuse and leave could be taken as an unwillingness to establish cordiality. To stay, but with a cup of coffee instead, is fine, but seeing how beer is such a part of Czech socialising, it ingratiates you to your hosts if you take part in their activities. Choose C, and proceed with moderation.

SITUATION THREE

After a few months here you've learned a bit of Czech and feel confident enough to use it when you need to. You are in a shop and need to ask the sales clerk something about the contents of a package, so you lurch into your question in broken Czech – yet she snaps something back at you that you cannot comprehend. Do you:

A Continue as well as you can, ignoring her rudeness, and vow to look up the words you don't know when you get home.

B Realise you can't make yourself understood, so start speaking English to her.

C Forget about it and go home.

Comments

Responses B and C are the ones you will probably prefer but may not be the best course of action. Speaking English to a shop assistant is likely a fruitless endeavour – not only will she probably not understand, she may not appreciate your assumption that she does. Of course, she may feel sympathy and try to help out, in which case you will have accomplished your task. If you just drop it, you'll get discouraged at your inability to communicate and at the unwillingness of the shop assistant to be helpful – in the 'down' phase of culture shock this is dangerous. Be bold and push through; choose A.

SITUATION FOUR

You are in a pub for lunch, where your waiter is particularly inattentive and rude. The 'fresh mixed salad' you order turns out to be sauerkraut from a jar, yet when you tell your server that this is not what you had in mind when you ordered, he only glares at you. Do you:

A Argue that this in fact is not fresh and send it back.

B Complain out of frustration, but accept it.

C Humbly accept the situation and realise that this is just how it is.

D Explain in reasonable terms that this is not what it claims to be, and that you would like an honestly fresh mixed salad.

Comments

Don't argue, and don't complain – with this approach, you're only yelling at a wall and will worsen the mood of both you and your server. Czechs themselves will most likely choose option C, feeling a bit intimidated by the prospect of a disagreement. If you can make it clear that they should be able to serve what they advertise, and can keep your cool about it, you just might be able to improve the situation for the next customers. The most common response is C, but try to assert your rights as a paying customer, and follow option D.

SITUATION FIVE

A male friend of yours makes a comment about women that offends your more progressive views (this could indeed happen whether you yourself are male or female). Do you:

A Tell him that a comment such as that is unacceptable in your country.

B Not respond and let it pass.

C Laugh along with it, not wanting to put a hurdle in your friendship.

D Explain as lightly as possible that you disagree and why, in hopes of changing his views.

Comments

Above all, remember that you are a visitor in his country, so any remark which smacks of cultural condescension will put him on the defensive. Meanwhile, not responding, or going along with it, will only encourage such remarks. If you can smile, yet shake your head and make a return comment, you will at least make it clear that you disapprove. The best response is D.

SITUATION SIX

You are in the midst of a seemingly interminable negotiation in which your company is trying to gain a lucrative deal with a Czech counter-part. You feel your offer is fair, yet the opposing number is waffling and coming up with further demands, which you find unacceptable. Do you:

A Sense that he will not relent and, seeing how important the deal is for you, realise that you will have to make more concessions.

B Go along with the slower pace, in hopes that he will finally accept your offer.

C Take charge of the situation by pointing out the advantages and disadvantages to both parties, and presenting what you believe is the fairest solution.

D Bully your way through with strong words, trying to out-tough your current rival/potential partner.

Comments

Remember that Czechs put a lot of value into personal understanding, so angry words and emotional displays are automatic deal breakers. Many Western businesspeople make the mistake of not recognising that Czechs often take some time to sort things out, all the while coming up with more ways to win. Patience is a virtue in negotiating, though without movement it can turn into a spiral. Therefore, by discussing circumstances in rational terms, maintaining friendly relations, you'll likely work toward a solution. The best response in this situation is C.

FURTHER READING

Books and Periodicals in English

The Prague Post, complete newspaper published every Wednesday.

The Prague Tribune, business and cultural news magazine.

Central European Business Weekly, a *Wall Street Journal*-type financial weekly.

Prague Business Journal, leading local business weekly.

The Fleet Sheet, brief newsletter rundown of the day's breaking news.

The Lands of the Czech Crown, a colourful and interesting bi-monthly magazine full of history and culture.

Pozor, hip cultural monthly magazine.

Literature

Czech literature, particularly that of the 20th century, is perhaps the most incisive commentary on life here during this tumultuous era.

Toward the Radical Center, Karel Čapek, Highland Park, NJ: Catbird Press, 1990. Čapek is one of the country's most prominent writers of the early 20th century. Written in a semi-absurdist, futuristic style, this is a "humorous and searching" insight to the root of human mysteries and contradictions. Also, *The War of the Newts*, Highland Park, NJ: Catbird Press, 1990.

The Good Soldier Švejk, Jaroslav Hašek, London: Penguin Books, 1973. Perhaps the most renowned work in Czech literature, both at home and abroad. Švejk (written as Sweik or Schweik in German and English) is the stereotypical non-conformist, beer-guzzling Czech, a reluctant soldier serving the Austro-Hungarian Empire. His rebellious adventures are shamelessly silly, while the underlying theme is a pointed analysis of Czech society.

The Dimension of the Present and other essays, Miroslav Holub, London: Faber and Faber, 1990. This renowned biologist/poet uses animal behaviour as his basis for a subtle criticism of government and society, as both a sociobiological theory and an allegory of survival under an oppressive regime. Also: *Poems Before and After,* Newcastle: Bloodaxe Books, 1990 – uses myth to enrich his politically charged commentary on life in the 1950s and 60s ('before' the Prague Spring uprising), and the 1970s and 80s ('after' the failed revolution).

The Little Town Where Time Stood Still, Bohumil Hrabal, London: Abacus 1993. Hrabal is another of the country's great writers, one who, like Václav Havel, stayed put and managed to get his politically conscious stories published. All his stories are subtle criticisms of political and social trends, the central characters of which search for far-reaching meaning in an isolated environment. Yet the mood is always light. Also: *Closely Observed Trains,* London: Abacus 1990; and *I Served the King of England,* London: Chatto & Windus, 1989.

Old Czech Legends, Alois Jirásek, London: Forest Books (UNESCO), 1992. Finally available in English, the very best collection of Czech myths, fairy tales, and half-truths, written by one of the giants of Czech 19th century literature.

The Spirit of Prague, Ivan Klíma, London: Granta Books, 1993. Collection of essays by this nationally acclaimed writer/journalist on events in Prague, dealing with critical events in each decade of his professional life: the 1940s and the Nazis, the 1950s and Stalin, the 1960s and the Prague Spring, the 1970s and Charter 77, the 1980s and the Velvet Revolution. Other works by Klíma touching similarly on life under Communism include *Love and Garbage* (London: Penguin, 1991); *My Golden Trades* (London: Penguin, 1992); and *Judge on Trial* (London: Vintage Books, 1992).

The Unbearable Lightness of Being, Milan Kundera, London: Faber and Faber, 1984. Probably the Czech Republic's most internationally well-known novelist, who consistently uses sex as a theme in his works. This is his best-known work, a probing, intimately personal look into human emotions and deeds, revealing a cry for freedom in a socially oppressive environment. Also (from the same publisher): *Life is Elsewhere*, 1986; *The Book of Laughter and Forgetting*, 1982; *Immortality*, 1991; and *The Farewell Party*, 1976 – the book backflap here says it best: "Milan Kundera poses serious questions with a blasphemous lightness which makes us understand that the modern world has taken away our right to tragedy."

Darkness Casts No Shadow, Arnošt Luštig, London: Quartet Books, 1976 and 1989. Harrowing account of life in Prague and in the concentration camp at Terezín (Theresienstadt) by this Czech Jew who survived the ordeal. Luštig made it to the US, where he has written and taught for many years; his other celebrated works include *Diamonds of the Night* and *Night and Hope*, both of which are similar to *Darkness Casts No Shadow* in their dark narrative.

Prague Tales, Jan Neruda, London: Chatto and Winders, 1993. Tales of life in Prague's Malá Strana quarter in the 19th century, funny and intimate.

The Engineer of Human Souls, Josef Škvorecký, London: Vintage Books, 1994. Škvorecký is one of the most important living Czech writers; he immigrated to Canada during the 1968 upheavals. This and several other of his works was banned in Czechoslovakia. As the subtitle explains, "an entertainment on the old themes of life, women, fate, dreams, the working class, secret agents, love, and death;" perhaps the most poignant depiction of life in Czechoslovakia under successive Nazi and Communist governments. The style is somehow so typically Czech: full of darkness and suffering, yet told in a blackly comical manner. Particularly recommended. Also: *The Republic of Whores,* London: Faber and Faber, 1994; *The Miracle Game,* London: Faber and Faber, 1991.

General History

Charles IV, the King from the Golden Cradle, Eduard Petiška, Prague: Martin Press, 1994. Full chronicle of King Charles IV and the Bohemian "Golden Age" of the mid-1300s, written by an eminent Czech historian. Literary and readable. Also: *A Treasury of Tales from the Kingdom of Bohemia*, 1994 – great book full of Czech lore, from Libuše to the Přemysls, plus lots of little-knowns.

History of Czechoslovakia in Outline, J.V. Polišenský, Prague: Bohemia International, 1991. Reprint of professor Polišenský´s excellent 1947 overview of the history of Czechoslovakia. Perhaps the best introduction to the subject, very readable and not too academic, though it leaves off at a critical point, just before the Communist takeover.

Contemporary History

We the People: the Revolutions in 1989 witnessed in Warsaw, Budapest, Berlin, and Prague, Timothy Garton Ash, London: Granta Books, 1990. An eyewitness account of the revolutions in Eastern Europe by an acclaimed British journalist.

So Many Heroes, Alan Levy, Sagaponack, NY: Second Chance Press, 1980. An update and reprint of the 1972 book *Rowboat to Prague*, a history of the 1968 Prague Spring witnessed by this noted journalist, who was subsequently expelled from the country.

Prague, in the Shadow of the Swastika, Callum McDonald and Jan Kaplan. Prague: Melantrich Press, 1995. Detailed history of the Nazi occupation of Prague, including the five-day Prague Uprising that marked the end of the Third Reich.

Stokes, Gale, *The Walls Came Tumbling Down: The Collapse of Communism in Eastern Europe*, Gale Stokes. Oxford: Oxford University Press, 1993. Textbook-like chronicle of all the political unrest in Eastern Europe from the 1968 Prague Spring, through the emergence of Charter 77, the 1989 Velvet Revolution, and the 1990-91 turbulence in Russia.

Social History and Commentary

The Origins of Backwardness in Eastern Europe, Daniel Chirot (ed.)
Berkeley: University of California Press, 1989. A poorly-timed
release (just before the revolutions throughout the region) which
nevertheless probes deeply into the history of political, social, and
even geographical problems in Russia, the Baltics, Poland, Czechoslovakia, Hungary, and the Balkans. It´s quite incisive into why
these nations have, for the the the better part of their histories, suffered
foreign domination and internal chaos.

The Gypsies of Eastern Europe, Daved Crowe and Kolsti Kohn, (eds.)
New York: M.E. Sharpe, Inc, 1991. Traces the history of migra-
tion of the Romany people, commonly referred to as Gypsies,
through eastern Europe, and deals with their culture and the
prejudices they encounter virtually everywhere they go.

How We Survived Communism and Even Laughed, Slavenka Drakulić.
London: Vintage Books, 1987. Touching and revealing description of life under Communism in the former Yugoslavia, the
themes of which apply equally to the Czech lands.

Disturbing the Peace, Václav Havel. London: Faber and Faber, 1990.
President Havel is a renowned philosopher, essayist, and playwright, with a keen perception of the evils of political oppression
and the position of human morality. This book looks back, with
Havel's admirable lack of bitterness, on the events of his life from
1968 to 1989; it is a testament to his method and ideology. Also:

Living in Truth, London: Faber and Faber, 1986 – A collection of deeply
philosophical essays which explicate one of his key concerns: living
a conscious and "truthful" life. Includes his famous open letter to
Gustáv Husák, for which he was sent to political prison.

Toward a Civil Society, Prague: Lidové Noviny Publishing House,
1995 – Selection of the president's political speeches.

Open Letters, London: Faber and Faber, 1991 – Open letters to the
Communist government, prose, and reflections from 1968-1990.
A good complement to *Disturbing the Peace*.

Letters to Olga, London: Faber and Faber, 1988, 1990, 1991 – Havel's prison correspondence with his late wife Olga, revealing not only his repressed political temperament, but also a touch of his personality.

Selected Plays, London: Faber and Faber, 1992 – Plays, many of which are absurdist, from 1963-1989.

Iron Curtain Rising, Peter Lanfer. San Francisco: Mercury House, 1991. An account that goes beyond the politics to examine the social and cultural trends in Eastern Europe. Examining how these differ between the former east and west European nations, the author provides timely insight on the future of this region; his notes on the former Yugoslavia have already proven accurate.

The Meaning of Czech History, Tomáš Garrigue Masaryk. Chapel Hill: University of North Carolina Press, 1974. Social analysis by the creator and first president of the Czechoslovak republic.

Revolutions in Eastern Europe: the Religious Roots, Niels Nielsen. Maryknoll, NY: Orbis Books, 1991. Traces the cutural, especially religious, roots, that spurned the former Soviet East Bloc to revolt.

Questions of Identity: Czech and Slovak Ideas of Nationality and Personality, Robert B. Pynsent. London: Central European University Press, 1994. Character study of Czechs and Slovaks.

The Czech Americans, Stephanie Sakson-Ford. New York: Chelsea House Publishers, 1989. Well researched book, one of dozens in this series, tracing the origins and development of Czech society in the US. Full of great old photos.

Art, Architecture, and Culture

A Guide to Czech and Slovak Glass, Diane E. Foulds. Prague: European Community Imports, Ltd., 1993. The complete story of glass and crystal manufacturing in the Czech and Slovak Republics, encompassing thorough explanations of what glass and crystal are and how they are made, the illustrious history of their production, and a shopping and shipping guide to all major glass-making towns and institutions.

Czechoslovakia, Erhard Gorys. London: Pallas Athene, 1991. Amazing in-depth study of the architectural history of the entire country – the very best guide to every castle, chateau, church, cathedral, tower, and wall of interest in the country.

The Czech Republic: Music in the Web of Life, Jana Marhounová. Prague: Empatie Publishers, 1993. Encompasses Czech music and its role in society, based on interviews with prominent Czech musicians, including pianist Rudolf Firkušny and composer Petr Eben.

Prague: Eleven Centuries of Architecture, a Historical Guide, Jaroslava Staňková; Jiří Štursa; and Svatopluk Voděra. Prague: PAV Publishers, 1992. The single best guide to every building of any architectural interest in Prague, including many that are no longer standing. A fascinating, thorough study.

Prague and Art Nouveau, Marie Vitochová; Jindřich Kejř; and Jiří Všetečka. Prague: V Ráji Publishing House, 1995. Beautifully photographed guide to the Art-nouveau style in Prague

Travel

Travel Adventure Guides: Prague and the Czech Republic, ITM Czech Republic in cooperation with ITM Canada, Prague, 1996. I humbly list this one first, because I wrote it.

The Rough Guide: Czech and Slovak Republics, The Rough Guides, London, 1996.

Lonely Planet Travel Survival Kit: Czech and Slovak Republics, Lonely Planet Publications, Melbourne, 1995.

Cadogan Guides: Prague, Cadogan Guides, London, 1996.

THE AUTHOR

Tim Nollen was raised and did most of his university work in Washington, DC. He learned both the ups and the downs of living abroad by spending a year with his family in London at age 12, and studying for a short time in Belgium. Perhaps it is the sum of these experiences that propelled him to return to Europe: after receiving a BA in philosophy, and thereby not feeling limited to a career launch, he has been occupied with various endeavors centered around the joy of foreign travel and living.

Tim first visited the Czech Republic in 1991, and a year later found himself here teaching English. He has continued his pursuit of a part-time career in music, studying at the Prague Conservatory and at Charles University. In recent years he has worked in the real estate business, though his interests continue to lie in travel and travel literature. Tim hits the road whenever possible—perpetual wanderlust has taken him to countries as diverse as Estonia, Jordan, and China, though always maintaining Prague as a base. Numerous articles of his have appeared in *The Prague Post*, and he is the author of *Prague and the Czech Republic: A Travel Adventure Guide*.

INDEX